Acknowledgements

Thank you to a friend at my church for giving up her time to read through my manuscript and offer editing suggestions.

Thank you to my parents, Lin and Paul, for introducing me to Christ from a young age and nurturing me in my Christian faith. Thank you for your unconditional love and support.

Thank you to my beautiful sister, Katrina, you are my greatest encourager.

Thank you to God for the gift of my two children. Thank you, Josh and Jess for providing me with material to use in this book.

Thank you to my incredible husband, Jason, for your constant support and help. You have played a huge part in making my dream a reality.

Thank you, Lord God, for giving me the dream of becoming a writer and for enabling me to write out of my experience of a relationship with you.

Vicki Cottingham

How to Use This Book

This is a one-year devotional, so the best time to begin is in January. However, as there are no dates in this book, the decision of when and where to start is down to the individual reader.

It is intended that one devotional is read each week, giving time to reflect and think on what has been read, and time to work on individual practical application (from the section "To Think About")

It can also be used in a small group. In which case the "To Think About" section can be used as an aid to discussion.

Contents

Trusting in God

Dear Friend,

"*Trust in the* LORD *with all your heart and lean not on your own understanding; in all your ways submit to him, and he will make your paths straight.*" **Proverbs 3:5-6** (NIV)

This was the introduction I wrote in my first blog:

I have mixed feelings as I begin this first entry of my first ever blog! Feelings of trepidation (love that word!) as I know so little about technology, (I only opened a Facebook account less than a year ago with the help of Jason, my husband, and Josh, my son) and also feelings of excitement because this blog encompasses two of my loves – writing and sharing truths that God has taught me.

I met with the Senior Minister at my church for a chat as I have just entered a new season. He brought up the suggestion that I might like to write a blog and, from the moment he mentioned it, I was gripped by the idea.

I have always loved writing. As a child I kept a diary and would write many stories. Now I keep a journal, so it seems a natural progression from these. As I said, I don't know much about technology so, before committing myself to blogging I spent time thinking and praying about it, and researching it … and here I am!

I recently had a huge decision to make as I believed God was telling me to step down from the church leadership team. I spent a long time asking God to confirm that I had heard him correctly. When I was sure, then I had to make the choice as to whether to be obedient to what he was asking of me.

He kept bringing to my attention the verses from **Proverbs 3:5-6** (NIV) *"Trust in the LORD with all your heart and lean not on your own understanding; in all your ways submit to him, and he will make your paths straight."*

I may not have fully understood what God was telling me, but I knew he was asking me to trust him. These verses have been important to me ever since my Granddad and Nan wrote them in the Bible they gave me when I was baptised at the age of eleven years.

These verses tell us that we are to do three things:

1. **Trust in God with all our heart** – it's inevitable that other people will let me down, just as there will be times when I will let others down, even if it may be unintentional. But God will never fail me; I can trust him because he loves me and wants the best for me.

2. **Don't lean on our own understanding** – when I have a decision to make I am very quick to rely on myself and what I think. The problem is my thinking doesn't always line up with God's thinking. My understanding is limited and I can't see into the future. God knows the end from the beginning. Rather than rely on my own understanding I need to rely on God and his Word.

3. **Submit to God** – that's hard! I like to be in control, or like to think I'm in control. But instead, I'm to hand over the control of my life to God. When I understand just how much God loves me, how much he has done for me and, as I've already said, that he wants the best for me, then I find it easier to submit to him.

If you and I do these three things, then we have a promise from God – that he will make our paths straight, or as it is written in the NLT "he will show you which path to take."

I find so much comfort in that promise. First, because God always keeps his promises, the truth in the Bible proves that, and secondly, because there is comfort and joy in knowing that God has a path already planned out for me if I choose to follow it.

He has a plan and a purpose for each of our lives. **Jeremiah 29:11** "For I know the plans I have for you," says the LORD. "They are plans for good and not for disaster, to give you a future and a hope."

I'm excited to put my hand into God's hand and have him lead me in the purpose he has designed me for, and I look forward as his plan for my life continues to unfold. I know it will be daunting at times, but I also know that he is with me every step of the way.

To Think About:

- *Will you also choose to trust God for your today and tomorrows?*

- *Will you choose to lean on him and submit to him?*

- *If you will do these things, he promises to show you the path to take.*

God Will Work Out His Plan for Your Life

Dear Friend,

As we are in the first month of a New Year, I have decided that I want to spend time alone with God, seeking what he wants for me this year. I have just gone through last year's journal to see how God has been with me, leading and preparing me for what will come this year. There was a verse I had written down in my journal last summer and God brought it to my attention again. It is **Psalm 138:8** in which David says

"The LORD will work out his plans for my life – for your faithful love, O LORD, endures forever. Don't abandon me, for you made me."

There are some wonderful truths and promises for us in just this one verse. Let's take a few minutes to look at them.

1. Our God is one who plans

I like to make plans. I plan out a weekly menu so I can then plan a shopping list. I make plans to go out with a friend for coffee. I make plans as to how I will spend the weekend. I plan to visit my sister in the coming school break. Everyone makes plans: plans for a wedding, a holiday, a night out with friends, planning a dinner party etc. However, when it comes to our plans, there is no guarantee that what we have planned and prepared for will actually happen. We can't plan for all eventualities, and sometimes circumstances are out of our control and disrupt our plans. Not so with God; he sees the end from the beginning; he knows the outcome. So when God plans for something it happens just as he planned.

"But the LORD's plans stand firm forever; His intentions can never be shaken."

Psalm 33:11

When Adam and Eve sinned in Genesis 3 God had already planned that he would send his son, Jesus, as the Saviour of the world (see Genesis 3:15) and 2,000 years later Jesus was born. For the Son of Man came to seek and save those who are lost." **Luke 19:10**. God has planned that we will one day live with him for eternity. We have that promise in **John 14:2-3** "There is more than enough room in my Father's home. If this were not so, would I have told you that I am going to prepare a place for you? When everything is ready, I will come and get you, so that you will always be with me where I am. "

2. God has a plan for your life.

Not only has God planned and promised a life with him for those who love him, he also has plans for your life, my life, and his plans for us are always for our good. "For I know the plans I have for you," says the LORD. "They are plans for good and not for disaster, to give you a future and a hope." **Jeremiah 29:11**. Have you asked God what his will is for your life? Do you have a dream, a goal, a desire to do something that you just know God has planned for you?

3. God's plans cannot be thwarted.

We have the promise that he **will** work out his plans for us. We can have confidence in God because he always does what he says he will do and he has the power to do it. We can trust him with our life. This is important because there will be days when the going is hard, when we feel that progress is slow, when circumstances are against us, and days when we question that it will ever work out. In those times we need to remember and rely on his promises to us. That's one of the reasons I keep a journal so that, particularly when it's tough, I can look back and remind myself of God's promises and his faithfulness.

4. God will make it happen.

God will work it out, not me, and not you. This requires humility on our part as we hand over control of our life and submit to his plan. It also requires patience as we wait for his timing to work things out. When God reveals his will and plans for us it doesn't necessarily mean that it will happen immediately. Often he takes us through a time of preparation, to make us ready. We need to learn to say, in your time Lord, not in mine; in your way, not my way. We can hold on to the promise that he will work it out. As God works it out we are not expected to sit back and take it easy, no, we are to keep trusting him, keep our focus on him and keep in tune to his leading and direction and demonstrate a willing obedience.

Like David, we can have confidence that God will work out his plan because God is a faithful and loving God. Nothing and no-one can take that love away from us. In **Romans 8:38-39** Paul says "And I am convinced that nothing can ever separate us from God's love. Neither death nor life, neither angels nor demons, neither our fears for today nor our worries about tomorrow—not even the powers of hell can separate us from God's love. No power in the sky above or in the earth below—indeed, nothing in all creation will ever be able to separate us from the love of God that is revealed in Christ Jesus our Lord." God is faithful to his Word and because he loves us, we can trust that his plan - his will for us - is right and good. God created us and he will complete the work that he has started in us, he stays the course, he will see it through to the finish. Paul writes "And I am certain that God, who began the good work within you, will continue his work until it is finally finished on the day when Christ Jesus returns." **Philippians 1:6**.

To Think About:

- *Have you asked God to show you what his plan, his will is for you?*

- *Do you trust in God and his plan for you?*

- *Do you trust God to work out his plan? Or are you trying to make it happen in your time and your way?*

- *What difference does knowing God has a plan for you make to the way you live?*

How Do You Define Success?

Dear Friend,

I have an ever growing list of favourite bible verses and sometimes God likes to grab my attention with a verse I've not really thought about much previously. He does this by making sure I've noticed, seen and read it two or three times. He's done this over the last few weeks of January with the following verse. It's a verse that I'm going to take for myself for the coming year and keep reminding myself of regularly.

"Commit to the Lord whatever you do, and he will establish your plans." **Proverbs 16:3** (NIV)

The Amplified Bible puts it like this:

"Roll your works upon the Lord (commit and trust them wholly to him, he will cause your thoughts to become agreeable to his will, and) so shall your plans be established and succeed."

God has created you and me, designed us specifically with personalities, gifts and abilities, strengths and weaknesses so that we can do the things he has planned for us to do. That's why it says in **Ephesians 2:10** "For we are God's masterpiece. He has created us anew in Christ Jesus, so we can do the good things he planned for us long ago."

It's these good things that God has called us to do and that we are to commit to him. We need to understand that Proverbs 16:3 is not about going to God with our plans, our dreams, our ideas about what we want to do and then expecting him to bless what we've already decided to do. Rather it's about learning from God what his plan is for us, committing it to God, placing it in his care and asking him to establish it.

What does it mean to commit these works to God? I believe it's about us letting go of them, rather than holding tightly onto them, handing over control to God. It's about trusting in his grace and love. Having the confidence to leave them in his care and safe-keeping, entrusting them to him, and being dependent and reliant on him. One way of doing this is by taking it to him in prayer and leaving it with him. We are only able to truly commit it to God when we have surrendered ourselves - our desires and our wants, and by submitting to him as Lord of our lives. Letting go is not easy; so often we want our own way, we want control, we want our say as to what is the best way to go about it. But when we do give it over to God, when we have first surrendered to God, something wonderful is able to happen.

The second part of the verse in Proverbs tells us what that is: "and he [that's God] will establish your plans." (NIV) or put another way: "and so shall your plans be established and succeed." (AMP)

What a wonderful promise! God is the one to establish our plans (those plans that are in keeping with his will). The world would have us believe that to be successful we need to have total control over our own lives, focus on what we want to achieve, not worry about hurting others when trying to reach the top, that the end justifies the means, etc.

But we learn from God's Word that true success comes when we surrender to God, when we commit our plans, our dreams, our works to him, and say, 'Lord, you are in control of this. My faith is in you and your will. I am confident that these things are safe in your care.' The only way to have our plans established and to experience success is to commit our work, our selves, everything to God. If you were to look up the word "established" in the thesaurus you would see the words achieve, succeed, thrive, and prosper. This is what God wants for each of us as we live and do the things he created us for. This is how one dictionary defines establish "to achieve success, so that people recognise your skill, qualities, or power". However, when our plans are established by God, others will recognise that our achievement is all because of him, that what we do points to God and brings him glory. We need to remember that it's not about us: it's all about him.

To Think About:

- *What do you think God may be telling you to commit to him so that he can establish it for you?*

  You may like to write out that verse in Proverbs 16 as a reminder and encouragement to you.

- *What steps do you need to put in place to take you to where God can establish your plans?*

You may find it helpful to share what you believe God wants you to do, with a close friend or mature Christian friend who can give some advice and make suggestions as well as support and encourage you. They can also help keep you on track and keep persevering.

An Attitude of Gratitude

Dear Friend,

Paul tells us in **1 Thessalonians 5:18** that we are to "Be thankful in all circumstances, for this is God's will for you who belong to Christ Jesus."

It's easy to be thankful when all is well with us, but it's another story when we are in the middle of difficult circumstances. If you are having a tough time right now, you may be thinking that you don't even want to read about being thankful. There's a part of me that would agree with you. Once I had made the decision that this week's devotional would be about giving thanks to God and having a gratitude attitude I hit a bump in the road.

I've been battling with depression for years and it regularly rears its ugly head. When it hits I don't really feel like being thankful and I certainly don't want to write about it! Besides, how can I write about something that I'm not doing? But I felt God was saying to go ahead and write it anyway. So I write even though I haven't yet achieved what I write about. And that's OK because being a Christian is about being on a journey; it's about our daily walk with God.

Whatever part of the journey you and I are on, the truth of God's Word does not change and we need to know God's truth. So, I am writing this for myself as much as I am writing it for you, and believe me, I know how challenging it is! The bible, especially the Psalms, is full of examples and exhortations to give thanks to God, David says in **Psalm 7:17** "I will give thanks to the LORD because of his righteousness; I will sing the praises of the name of the LORD Most High." (NIV).

Expressing gratitude to God is an act of the will; it's a choice we can make regardless of how we feel. Expressing gratitude may not change our circumstances, but it will change our hearts. If I focus on my problems and difficulties, the bigger they seem and the worse I feel. Then it's almost impossible to express any gratitude to God because my feelings have taken over control and I have allowed them to do so.

Instead, I need to make the choice that I will give thanks to God. There is so much I can give thanks to God for: his constant presence with me, his strength, his love, my life in him, my husband who is fulfilling his vow to love me "in sickness and in health", my children, my home, the food I eat and the clothes I wear, friends to laugh and share with, the close relationship I share with my sister and my parents, my love of reading and writing, a bible to read, and the list goes on...

A wonderful thing begins to happen, as I choose to give thanks, as I choose to express an attitude of gratitude. I actually begin to feel more grateful and begin to see more clearly just how much I have to be grateful for. God has given me so much and it's easy to forget it or take it for granted. That's why I need to choose to live my life with an attitude of gratitude, and the more I exercise this attitude, the healthier that attitude, and I, will be.

Positive thinking and reading self-help books won't give us the power to live a life of gratitude. The good news is, we have been given the Holy Spirit and he is the one who gives us the power we need to make the choice to express the gratitude attitude.

To Think About:

- *Ask God to help you develop an attitude of gratitude despite your difficult circumstances and the way you may be feeling.*

- *Take some time out with God and give him your thanks for all he has given you. Be specific. Include everything the Holy Spirit brings to your mind. For example, if you're thankful for a particular relationship, tell him why you're thankful.*

- *What happens when you do this?*
  Read Psalm 103 as an aid to expressing your gratitude to God.

God Doesn't Have A 'B Team'

Dear Friend,

My son, Josh, decided in this, his last year at secondary school to try out for the school football team. He was thrilled when he was told that he had a place on the 'B Team'. His skills weren't quite up to the standard of the 'A Team', but that didn't matter to us. All that mattered was he'd gone for it and given it his best. He was happy and we were happy for him.

It started me thinking about how we all have a need for acceptance and that for most things in life we have to meet a standard or a set of criteria in order to be accepted, for example, when applying for a new job, joining a team or club. Josh is applying for Sixth Form College and has an interview in February. Acceptance into college will be dependent on his application form, his interview and his exam grades.

We learn about acceptance and rejection early in life. It starts in the home for the child who is accepted with the unconditional love of the parent. However, some parents give the child the message that they are only accepted if they live up to their parents' expectations or if their appearance is a particular way or they have a certain character. These messages are reinforced at school as we each long to be accepted and welcomed by our peers, and if we aren't accepted we have to deal with the pain of rejection.

With our need for acceptance and approval and our fear of rejection, we can bend ourselves out of shape trying to fit in and be who others want us to be and we can wear ourselves out by trying to reach impossible standards.

We can take this mind-set with us into our relationship with God. We think that he will only accept us if we prove that we are "good Christians" by doing the things we think we should do. We think that if we mess up then God is going to reject us. We think there's no way he could love me, I'm not good enough, not clever enough, not sporty enough etc.

The good news is that God does accept you and me unconditionally because he loves us. Paul writes in **Romans 5:7** "Therefore, accept each other just as <u>Christ has accepted you</u> so that God will be given glory."

In **Ephesians 1:4-5** we read "Even as [in His love] <u>He chose us</u> <u>[actually picked us out for Himself as His own]</u> in Christ before the foundation of the world, that we should be holy (consecrated and set apart for Him) and blameless in His sight, even above reproach, before Him in love. For He foreordained us (destined us, planned in love for us) to be adopted (revealed) as <u>His own</u> <u>children</u> through Jesus Christ, in accordance with the purpose of His will [because it pleased Him and was His kind intent]" (Amp)

Paul says in his letter to the Romans "Who will accuse those whom God has <u>chosen</u>? God has <u>approved</u> of them." **Romans 8:33.** (GWT)

We read in another of Paul's letters, "We know, dear brothers and sisters, that God <u>loves</u> you and has <u>chosen</u> you to be his own people." **1 Thessalonians 1:4.**

And in John's first letter he writes, "<u>God showed how much he loved</u> <u>us</u> by sending his one and only Son into the world so that we might have eternal life through him. This is real love—not that we loved God, but that he loved us and sent his Son as a sacrifice to take away our sins." **1 John 4:9-10.**

These are just some of the verses in the bible that tell us God loves us, that he chose us and has accepted us. What we need to understand is that God doesn't choose us on the basis of who we are or because of anything we have done. Each one of us needs to come to the place of realising that there is nothing we can possibly do to earn his acceptance and love. <u>His acceptance of us is based on who he is.</u> He chose us because he loves us; God is love, that's his essential nature.

His love for us is constant; he doesn't say I accepted you yesterday, but today's another matter, I no longer accept you, you've messed up too many times, I've had it with you. Nothing can ever happen to make him remove his love from us. His love for us is steadfast, there is nothing we can do to make him love us more than he does at this very moment and there is nothing we can do to make him love us less than he does right now. It's worth repeating that his acceptance is not based on who we are, or try to be, on what we do or don't do. His acceptance of us is based on who God is, that's why we can have complete confidence and trust in him. He never rejects or turns away anyone who comes to him. When we realise that we don't need to earn his acceptance and love, then we are freed from the burden that comes with always trying to earn it and we are free to enjoy his love and acceptance and love him in return. It says in **1 John 4:19** "We love Him because He first loved us." (NKJV)

One last thing, God doesn't have an 'A Team' and 'B Team' (as Joshua's school has with football). God accepts each one of us completely, there is no first class and second-class Christians. We are all on his 'A Team'. In **Colossians 3:11** we read "In this new life, it doesn't matter if you are a Jew or a Gentile, circumcised or uncircumcised, barbaric, uncivilized, slave, or free. Christ is all that matters, and he lives in all of us." God says to you and to me,

I've chosen you and love you, and I've got a place for you in my family that can only be filled by you.

To Think About:

- *Ask God to help you know in your heart, as well as believe in your head, that he has accepted and chosen you because he loves you so very much.*

- *What difference does it make to your outlook and actions when you know that you are accepted by God?*

- *How can you show God's love and acceptance to others in your church family?*

Can You See the Family Resemblance?

Dear Friend,

One Sunday morning after the church service I was chatting over coffee with a lady and a mutual friend. When she saw Jess she said how much my daughter looks like me and my friend added that we have the same character too. She's not the first one to say how much my daughter looks like me.

I know that on several occasions I've said to Josh, my son, "Oh, you're just like your father!" when he acts in a certain way. It's no surprise that there are these family resemblances, after all, being family means we have the same DNA. People also say that you become like the person you live with.

Not only do we all have a physical family, we are also given a spiritual family when we become a Christian. God adopts us into his family and we become children of God. "God decided in advance to adopt us into his own family by bringing us to himself through Jesus Christ. This is what he wanted to do, and it gave him great pleasure." **Ephesians 1:5**. With our adoption God also gives us new life, "This means that anyone who belongs to Christ has become a new person. The old life is gone; a new life has begun!" **2 Corinthians 5:17** and with our new life he gives us the gift of his Holy Spirit living within us, his DNA, if you like, "And now you Gentiles have also heard the truth, the Good News that God saves you. And when you believed in Christ, he identified you as his own by giving you the Holy Spirit, whom he promised long ago. The Spirit is God's guarantee that he will give us the inheritance he promised and that he has purchased us to be his own people. He did this so we would praise and glorify him." **Ephesians 1:13-14**.

Just as Jess, my daughter, resembles me in character, we too, as sons and daughters of God, are to resemble Jesus Christ. In **Romans 8:29** we read "God, in his foreknowledge, chose them <u>to bear the family likeness of his Son</u>, that he might be the eldest of a family of many brothers [and sisters]. He chose them long ago; when the time came he called them, he made them righteous in his sight, and then lifted them to the splendour of life as his own sons [and daughters]." (Phillips)

People should be able to see something of Jesus in you and me as they look at us, as they watch the way we behave, the way we speak and the way we are with our spiritual family. For some, we will be the only Jesus that they get to see and this should motivate us to resemble him more and more. As we continue to learn how much God loves us, we also grow to love him more deeply and as our love for him grows, we will love others as God loves them and they will begin to recognise it as God's love in us. By loving others, we are living our life as Jesus lived his. "We know how much God loves us, and we have put our trust in his love. God is love, and all who live in love live in God, and God lives in them. And as we live in God, our love grows more perfect. So we will not be afraid on the day of judgment, but we can face him with confidence <u>because we live like Jesus here in this world</u>." **1 John 4:16-17**.

We obey God and follow his will and live as he wants us to live, not out of fear, but out of our love for him. "All who keep His commandments [who obey His orders and follow His plan, live and continue to live, to stay and] abide in Him, and He in them. [They let Christ be a home to them and they are the home of Christ.] And by this we know and understand and have the proof that _He [really] lives and makes His home in us_: by the [Holy] Spirit Whom He has given us." **1 John 3:24** (AMP)

We have God's gift of the Holy Spirit within us and it's his work to grow us to become more like Christ. This doesn't mean we just sit back and do nothing, no, we are to work in partnership with him and we do this by providing an environment in which he can do his work. It begins with having the right attitude and choosing to submit to God, this is the healthy environment which gives him the room to grow the character of Christ in us so that we become more and more like Christ. **Galatians 5:22-23** "_the fruit of the [Holy] Spirit [the work which His presence within accomplishes] is love, joy (gladness), peace, patience (an even temper, forbearance), kindness, goodness (benevolence), faithfulness, Gentleness (meekness, humility), self-control (self-restraint, continence)._" (Amp) Our growth is stunted when we refuse to allow the Holy Spirit to do his work in us.

It's my desire this year that I will increasingly show a family resemblance to my Heavenly Father so that when people get to know me they will say "You are just like your Father; I know whose family you belong to." What's your desire?

To Think About:

- *Take an honest look at yourself, are you living just like Jesus? What may be hindering you from doing this? How do you think the Holy Spirit can help in this area?*

- *Look back on your experiences over the past week or so and ask God if there's one aspect of the fruit of the Holy Spirit (Galatians 5:22-23) that he wants to grow in you. Are you willing for this to happen?*

Aspects of Love

Dear Friend,

As I write this, Valentine's Day is approaching so it will probably come as no surprise to you that I have chosen to write about love. I'm not talking about the romantic, sentimental, bunch-of-roses, box-of-chocolates kind of love. I'm talking about authentic, genuine, godly love. It's a love based not just on feelings because it's not just a matter of the heart. To love is a choice, it's a matter for the mind, an act of will. We are to love consistently, whether we feel like it or not, whether the person reciprocates in love or not, and we should not use it or abuse it to manipulate others.

We read in **1 John 4:8** "But anyone who does not love does not know God, for God is love." God loves us with a love that we have never ever experienced before, and as we follow him and love him in return, his love flows through us to others. Jesus, the Son of God, says to us "So now I am giving you a new commandment: Love each other. Just as I have loved you, you should love each other." **John 13:34**. As I wrote last week, we are to become more like Jesus, he's our role model.

There's a great description of authentic, genuine, godly love in **1 Corinthians 13:4-8** "4 Love is patient, love is kind. It does not envy, it does not boast, it is not proud. 5 It does not dishonour others, it is not selfseeking, it is not easily angered, it keeps no record of wrongs. 6 Love does not delight in evil but rejoices with the truth. 7 It always protects, always trusts, always hopes, always perseveres. 8 Love never fails." (NIV)

This is how God loves us and it describes for us the kind of love we are to have for one another, whether it's between husband and wife, mother and child, with our parents, siblings, friends etc. This kind of love is applicable and relevant to any and every relationship.

So how does that translate to my life today? What does it mean for me to love others in this way? In order to understand it better I've paraphrased these verses on love below after meditating on them during the week. As I paraphrased them I found it helpful to keep someone in mind. For me it made sense to consider my relationship with Jason, my husband. Here's what I came up with...

Love makes allowances for each other, it accepts and appreciates our differences, it is slow to speak and quick to listen.

Love is gentle, gracious and considerate of the needs and interests of others, it is not overbearing, demanding things be done in a certain way (my way).

Love rejoices in others' achievements and gifting, it gives others genuine praise, it does not harbour resentment or long for what others have.

Love does not say 'Look at me, look what I can do', it does not brag nor puff up self, rather it seeks to build others up and encourage them.

Love is not arrogant or conceited, it does not have an inflated ego, instead it recognises the value and worth of others.

Love treats others with respect; it uses words to speak positively, words that encourage and supports others. It does not gossip, criticise or insult others.

Love is not about looking out for number one, getting the best for myself; instead it looks to give its best to others, to be outward rather than inward looking.

Love is self-controlled, peace-loving and calm; it is not bad-tempered, not irritable and does not take its frustrations and annoyances out on others.

Love keeps forgiving and does not hold a grudge; neither does it bring up previous offences at any opportunity.

Love delights when others pursue the will of God for their lives; it takes no delight in anything that causes pain to others.

Love does all it can to keep the relationship safe, it defends and guards the relationship, and lets nothing come between it.

Love has confidence and faith in each other, it relies and leans on each other, and it is committed to each other.

Love believes the best about each other and for each other, it looks forward to a lifetime together, believing that each can be all that God intends them to be.

Love is constant, it doesn't give up at the first sign of trouble, it endures and goes from strength to strength as difficulties are overcome.

This kind of love is never defeated, it doesn't die, rather this kind of love succeeds, it prospers, it thrives, it flourishes.

Praise God! (Just felt it needed a shout of praise right there!)

Having shared it with you, now I want to spend some more time on my own with God, thinking about it. It's all very well knowing what love is all about, but I can't just leave it there. It's just as important to discover ways in which I can demonstrate this kind of love to my husband (and to others). That's why James writes in **James 1:22** "But don't just listen to God's word. You must do what it says. Otherwise, you are only fooling yourselves." I'm also going to use what I wrote about love as a prayer to God, asking him to help me love others in this way, because I know very well I can't do it on my own.

To Think About:

- *Is there one aspect of love (from 1 Corinthians 13:4-8) that you feel God is prompting you to develop?*

- *Is God bringing to your mind someone he wants you to love in this way?*

- *How could you paraphrase those verses so that they become more relevant to you? You might like to write them out as a poem to give to your spouse, or your friend, or someone else.*

How Deeply Rooted Are You?

Dear Friend,

A friend was telling me recently that one of their trees in the garden, a big tree with many roots, had been blown over, uprooted by the recent strong winds we had been experiencing. I voiced my surprise that this had happened if it had many roots but my friend explained that it was because the roots had been just under the surface rather than going deep in the soil. Deep roots are what helps a tree to withstand storms and keep secure.

Do you know that the bible likens us to trees? It says in **Psalm 1:3** that: "Those who meditate on God's word and delight in it are like trees: They are like trees planted along the riverbank, bearing fruit each season. Their leaves never wither, and they prosper in all they do."

The Amplified Bible puts it like this: "And he shall be like a tree firmly planted [and tended] by the streams of water, ready to bring forth its fruit in its season; its leaf also shall not fade or wither; and everything he does shall prosper [and come to maturity]."

Are you "firmly planted [and tended]"? If you and I are it means that although we will still experience storms in our life, we are more able to withstand them, and not be uprooted by them because we are securely rooted and have anchorage.

So what or who do we need to be rooted in? **Jeremiah 17:7-8a** tells us "But blessed are those who trust in the Lord and have made the Lord their hope and confidence. They are like trees planted along a riverbank, with roots that reach deep into the water. Such trees are not bothered by the heat or worried by long months of drought. Their leaves stay green, and they never stop producing fruit."

This tells me that we need to be rooted in God, he is the source of our faith, our hope, our confidence, he is the one in whom we trust. We can rely on him to help us withstand any storm. We are secure in him and he provides us with stability. The verse mentioned earlier in Psalm 1 also tells us that we need to be rooted in God's Word – meditating and delighting in it.

Paul writes to the Ephesians about being deeply rooted in love and having love as our firm foundation, grounded in the love God has for us and gives us. "May He grant you out of the rich treasury of His glory to be strengthened and reinforced with mighty power in the inner man by the [Holy] Spirit [Himself indwelling your innermost being and personality]. May Christ through your faith [actually] dwell (settle down, abide, make His permanent home) in your hearts! May you be rooted deep in love and founded securely on love" **Ephesians 3:16-17**.

When Paul writes to the Colossians he again uses the imagery of a rooted tree to explain that we are to be securely and deeply rooted in Christ. "Have the roots [of your being] firmly and deeply planted [in Him, fixed and founded in Him], being continually built up in Him, becoming increasingly more confirmed and established in the faith, just as you were taught, and abounding and overflowing in it with thanksgiving." **Colossians 2:7** (AMP).

The roots of a tree absorb water and other nutrients from the soil to feed the tree so that it can grow to maturity. So too for us, being rooted in Christ, connected with him, will help us to grow to spiritual maturity. The Holy Spirit within us gives us the power and resources we need so that we flourish and grow to become all that God intended us to be. No one sees the roots, they are hidden in Christ, but the evidence of them should be seen - as we grow in our faith, as we love others as Christ loves us, as we trust and rely on him, as we feed on his Word, as we live with confidence and hope and as others see how we respond and keep standing despite whatever storm we are experiencing.

To Think About:

- *What "storms of life" have you experienced?*

- *What has enabled you to keep standing?*

- *How can you, in practical terms, keep yourself rooted in Christ?*

Healthy Boundaries

Dear Friend,

As parents, Jason and I are responsible for our children's well-being. That's why we, like many parents, set boundaries for our children. One of those boundaries is the time they are to go to bed. They sometimes moan that everyone else their age goes to bed much later than they do. My response to that is that I'm not responsible for other people's children, but I am responsible for them and that means setting an age appropriate bedtime. I believe that it's important for their health and for them to get a good night's sleep so that they can concentrate in their classes. They may not agree with me, but I don't do this to be unfair or mean or because I don't care. In fact, the opposite is true: I do it because I love them and want the best for them.

I remember Josh saying when he reached the age of fifteen years that now he could watch fifteen-rated films. We talked about it and I explained that, while in the eyes of the law he is allowed to watch these films, he is still under Jason's and my responsibility and care. So if we feel that a certain film will be harmful to his soul and mind, then we will decide that he is not to watch it. Again, he may not see it from that perspective, he may think we are being unfair and unreasonable, and that we are looking for ways to make his life miserable. Whereas the truth is that we are looking out for him and that we have good reasons for the boundaries we set. God has placed our children in our care and we are accountable to him for our parenting.

God, as our Heavenly Father, parents each one of us in the same way. He sets boundaries for us, such as the rules and standards that we are to live by. He has made it clear in his word what his boundaries are in areas such as marriage, parenting, work ethic, finance, etc. Like children, we sometimes rebel against these boundaries. We think we know best, we think God's unfair, that he's being deliberately mean, that he's taking the joy out of everything. These are not the reasons God has set boundaries. God has set these boundaries because he loves and cares about us. He wants what is good for us and he wants us to enjoy the best possible life within the limits he sets, and these limits are not narrow.

Let's take a moment to look at the beginning of the Bible with Adam and Eve. They are the only people to have known a perfect world, heaven on earth. God placed them in a wonderful garden and gave them the responsibility to take care of his creation. They had an incredible relationship with God which had no barriers. There was a wonderful harmony. God had given them everything they could ever need and the boundaries he set were wide. "15 The LORD God placed the man in the Garden of Eden to tend and watch over it. 16 But the LORD God warned him, 'You may freely eat the fruit of every tree in the garden— 17 except the tree of the knowledge of good and evil. If you eat its fruit, you are sure to die.'" **Genesis 2:15-17**. However, they chose to cross the boundary set by God. They became dissatisfied with what they had. They thought they knew better than God. They thought he was being unfair and they chose to do the one thing God had told them not to do. "6 The woman was convinced. She saw that the tree was beautiful and its fruit looked delicious, and she wanted the wisdom it would give her. So she took some of the fruit and ate it. Then she gave some to her husband, who was with her, and he ate it, too. 7 At that moment their eyes were opened, and they suddenly felt shame at their nakedness. So they sewed fig leaves together to cover themselves." **Genesis 3:6-7**.

Their choice to disobey God and cross the boundary led to serious consequences. No longer was their world perfect, sin and death had been introduced to their world, their relationship with God was broken, their relationship with each other was damaged and creation was affected.

Let's be honest here - there have been times when we can see ourselves, our attitudes and actions, in Adam and Eve. Haven't there been times when we felt we knew better than God? We tell ourselves we deserve the best, our life is our own therefore it's up to us to set our own boundaries. We tell ourselves we're not hurting anyone. If we listen to these kind of thoughts for too long, then our choice to disobey is quick to follow. However, we then have to face the serious consequences: a broken relationship with God, damaged relationships with others, pain, hurt, guilt and the death of our peace and joy.

Living within the boundaries set for us by God is so much better for us. It is within his boundaries that we experience a blessed life and the life that God intends for us to enjoy. We are reconciled to God and to others; there is love, joy, hope, peace and purpose. They are the consequences of keeping within God's boundaries. In **John 10:10** Jesus says "The thief [the devil] comes only in order to steal and kill and destroy. I came that they may have and enjoy life, and have it in abundance (to the full, till it overflows)." (Amp). That's the life that God has prepared for those who keep inside the boundaries he has set for us. It's a mistake and a lie of the devil to think that this kind of life can be enjoyed and experienced outside of God's boundaries.

We all at times have crossed God's boundaries, but the way back is simple: it's to recognise our sin, come before God and confess it to him. God has promised to forgive us and he welcomes us back into his presence. **1 John 1:9** tells us that "But if we confess our sins to him, he is faithful and just to forgive us our sins and to cleanse us from all wickedness."

When we really believe that God, our heavenly father, has provided us with these boundaries because he loves us and wants us to experience his best for us, then the choice of where we will live our lives - within or outside of his boundaries - becomes easier.

To Think About:

- *When have you chosen to cross the boundaries God has set for you and what have been the consequences of this decision?*

- *Consider a time when you chose to keep inside the boundaries God has set for you. What have been the consequences of this?*

- *What part do you think your attitude towards God has to play in how you respond to God's boundaries?*

When it seems like God is taking everything away from you

Dear Friend,

When I was first diagnosed with M.E (Myalgic Encephalomyelitis) in the late 1990s I really struggled to come to terms with it. I can remember in the early years, when it was at its worst, saying that God was taking everything away from me. This was truly how I felt, and the hurt and the pain from what I was losing was intense. It's a pain which actually cannot fully be put into words. Not only had I lost my health and strength, I had to give up work and I wasn't able to do the things I'd been doing at church, such as leading Sunday School and running a youth group with my husband. Jason and I had married in the Summer of 1995 and the illness meant I wasn't able to do all I wanted to do in the home or to be the kind of wife I wanted to be for Jason and I wasn't able to socialise. For me that meant not going to church and mixing with church friends. It really felt like God was taking everything away from me and like I said, it was extremely painful.

From books I've read and conversations I've had with others, I know I'm not alone in feeling like this. Perhaps you have gone through a similar experience which has caused you to feel as though God is taking everything away from you or perhaps you're going through it right now.

Job must have had similar feelings when he lost his wealth, children, health, his standing in the city as an elder and on top of all this he lost his wife's support and the respect of his friends. (You can read his story in the book of Job in the bible). And yet, he was still able to say at one point "*I came naked from my mother's womb, and I will be naked when I leave. The LORD gave me what I had, and the LORD has taken it away. Praise the name of the LORD!*" **Job 1:21**.

Although I felt like God was taking everything away from me, he never removed his presence. I knew him with me all the time and he taught me a valuable lesson through this trial that I'm not sure I would have learnt otherwise.

It's all too easy to focus our life all about the things we have and the things we do. I can tend to lean on these things and people instead of depending on God. My relationship with God had suffered too because I was too busy doing things for him and depending on my own ability and strength to serve him in church.

It was through the loss, the pain, and the trials that God taught me that he is all I need. Through one loss after another God taught me that these things are not dependable; I can't depend on my health, on myself, on what I have and what I do, but I can totally depend on God. When I was able to do almost nothing, I found I was able to meet with God, have quality time with him, learn from him, and get to know him and love him on a much deeper level than I had had time for before. He taught me to trust him, to lean on him and wholly depend on him.

The Psalmist was able to say: "*This I declare about the Lord: He alone is my refuge, my place of safety; he is my God, and I trust him.*" **Psalm 91:2**.

Paul too learnt what it meant to rely on God. In his letter to the Corinthians he wrote "*We think you ought to know, dear brothers and sisters, about the trouble we went through in the province of Asia. We were crushed and overwhelmed beyond our ability to*

endure, and we thought we would never live through it. In fact, we expected to die. But as a result, we stopped relying on ourselves and learned to rely only on God, who raises the dead."
1 Corinthians 1:8-9

It was not until I reached the point, from losing so much, when I felt God was all I had, that I then found God to be all I need. I believe that's what he wants for all his children. I'd like to be able to tell you that once I'd learnt that lesson I never needed to learn it again, but that's not the case. Since then, every so often, I need to re-learn it and God has led me through a few experiences when I've needed to be taught again by him to trust and lean on him alone and to know that he is all I need.

Because of Job's experiences he was able to say at the end to God "I had heard of You [only] by the hearing of the ear, but now my [spiritual] eye sees You." **Job 42:5** (AMP) It's the difference between knowing about God in our heads and really knowing him in our hearts. It's all about a close, day by day, moment by moment, relationship with him.

While I can't say I'm glad to have M.E and all the problems that go with it, I am glad that God loves me so much and cares enough about me to use the experience to work in my life and to draw me closer to him. This time will then not have been wasted.

I know that whatever you may have been through or are going through is so very painful, the depth of which cannot fully be put in words, but I pray that through it you may know that God is with you, that he hasn't abandoned you and that he is saying to you, "Trust me, lean on me, I won't let you down, I am all that you need." I also pray that when God has brought you through it you, like Job, will be able to say "But he knows where I am going. And when he tests me, I will come out as pure as gold. For I have stayed

on God's paths; I have followed his ways and not turned aside."
Job 23:10-11

To Think About:

- *Take some time out to read the whole story of Job.*

- *What do you think God has been wanting to say to you through your painful experience?*

- *I would encourage you to journal your experiences, including how you feel about them and to also record what God is saying to you in them. I find it so helpful to do this and it's good to look back over them when you feel the need to.*

Why Now, God?

Dear Friend,

While trying to come to terms with the diagnosis that I was suffering with M.E I can remember asking God "Why now?" Why now when I'm in the early years of marriage to Jason and we are still adjusting to the relationship? Why now when I'm busy with church activities? Why now when, in my twenties, I should be fit and healthy and able to go out to work and make a financial contribution to our marriage? I told God that now is just not a good time to have to deal with a long-term illness.

I didn't realise it at the time but what I was actually saying to God was: "You know what? You've got it wrong, I shouldn't be ill now. You've made a mistake and I'm going to tell you why you're wrong." I thought I knew what was best for my life. Surely I knew better than God what I needed and when I needed it. I had forgotten that God is my Creator and I am his created one. I had forgotten that he is the potter and I am the clay. "And yet, O LORD, you are our Father. We are the clay, and you are the potter. We all are formed by your hand." **Isaiah 64:8**

God used the example of a potter and clay to say this to Jeremiah: "Up on your feet! Go to the potter's house. When you get there, I'll tell you what I have to say.' So I went to the potter's house, and sure enough, the potter was there, working away at his wheel. Whenever the pot the potter was working on turned out badly, as sometimes happens when you are working with clay, the potter would simply start over and use the same clay to make another pot. Then GOD's Message came to me: 'Can't I do just as this potter does, people of Israel?' GOD's Decree! 'Watch this potter. In the same way that this potter works his clay, I work on you, people of Israel.'" **Jeremiah 18:1-6** (The Message)

God is the potter and you and I are the clay. God, the potter, shapes us according to his plan and even before he begins shaping he knows his intended outcome. He has a purpose for each of us and so shapes and reshapes us using what he wants to make us fit for that purpose. He knows what is best for us because he created us and because he loves us. So he works on us, moulding, bending, shaping and transforming.

One day God answered my "Why now?" with a question for me. He said if not now, then when? As I considered this question of when (in my opinion) it would be a good time, God helped me to understand that there is never a 'good time' to face a long-term illness. Just as there is never a good time for your husband to say he doesn't love you any more and for him to walk out on you. Just as there's never a good time to be told the cancer which you thought was in remission has returned. Just as there's never a good time for your teenage daughter to come home after school one day and tell you she's pregnant. Just as there's never a good time to face bankruptcy. There's never a good time to face any kind of trial or difficulty.

God has shown me that although there is never a good time to go through difficulty, there is a right time to go through it and that right time is known only to God. He's the one who knows the end from the beginning and he's the one who holds time in his hands. God says "I make known the end from the beginning, from ancient times, what is still to come. I say, 'My purpose will stand, and I will do all that I please.'" **Isaiah 46:10** (NIV). When I know the truth that God is love and he loves me, that he is good and wants only the best for me, that he has everything under control, then I can begin to put my trust in him and I can rest in him, knowing that if God is allowing me to go through this difficult trial then it is the right time for me to go through it, even if I never understand why. I can have the security of knowing that I will never have to go through it alone - he will be with me every step of the way. Not only can I lean on his promise to be with me, I know that he will also give me the strength and grace I need to be an overcomer.

If you know and love God, then whatever trial you are going through has first been Father-filtered by him. What do I mean by that? I mean that it has passed through the loving hands of God our Father who knows just how much we can handle, if only we will place ourselves in his loving care.

A better question for me to ask God is not "Why now?" but "What now?" During the trial how can I glorify God? How do I live in such a way as to not waste the experience? It doesn't mean I'm resigned to the difficult situation or that I lose hope of life ever changing. It does, however, mean that I accept it. I accept that God knows what he's doing even if I don't know. It means I willingly hand over the control of my life to him and I trust him with everything. Only when I understand that God loves me, that he wants the best for me, that his purpose is not to bring me down but to build me up, am I able to accept that all that comes into my life, whether good or bad, comes just at the right time.

To Think About:

- *If you're in the midst of a trial, why not tell God everything, your thoughts and your feelings, be completely honest with him. By doing so, you will be opening up an opportunity for him to reveal himself to you in a deeper way. You can begin to connect with him in a way that perhaps you've never known before.*

- *What have you learned about yourself and about God during a trial or when you've looked back over it?*

- *Have you come to the point when you can say to God "What now?"*

- *During the coming week take time to meditate on **1 Peter 1:6-7** 'So be truly glad. There is wonderful joy ahead, even though you have to endure many trials for a little while. ⁷ These trials will show that your faith is genuine. It is being tested as fire tests and purifies gold—though your faith is far more precious than mere gold. So when your faith remains strong through many trials, it will bring you much praise and glory and honour on the day when Jesus Christ is revealed to the whole world."*

Trust to Luck or Trust in God?

Dear Friend,

Ever had one of those times when it seems that one thing after another goes wrong?

At the end of last year our heating broke down and we needed to call the plumber. Early on in this year Jason's car had a service as it had a major problem. We thought we had it all sorted when, in only a matter of days, another problem with the car surfaced so it needed fixing again and then last Sunday it broke down as Jason and my son, Josh, were leaving church after the morning service. I couldn't believe it when Jason rang me to let me know what had happened and asked me to come and pick them up as his car was going nowhere!

I was annoyed to have something else go wrong, especially when we had anticipated an enjoyable afternoon with friends. As I said, it was one thing after another and I'd had enough! Where was God in all this? How could he let this happen? Didn't he know the effect it was having on us to cope with one problem after another? I was thoroughly fed up and discouraged. Jason, on the other hand, had a great attitude in it all. At least one of us did.

When the breakdown truck (finally!) arrived, the guy said to Jason more than once how lucky we were. If Jason had been driving at a fast speed when it happened, the back of the car could have broken right off causing a terrible accident. When I heard that, my perspective on it all changed, not because I believe in luck, chance or fate or anything like that, but because it made me realise that God really was in it all. He was watching over us, keeping us safe and protecting us from real harm. If God hadn't been with us I dread to think what could have happened.

He knows exactly what he is doing and he knows just how many trials and difficulties to allow into our lives. "For no temptation (no trial regarded as enticing to sin), [no matter how it comes or where it leads] has overtaken you and laid hold on you that is not common to man [that is, no temptation or trial has come to you that is beyond human resistance and that is not adjusted and adapted and belonging to human experience, and such as man can bear]. But God is faithful [to His Word and to His compassionate nature], and He [can be trusted] not to let you be tempted and tried and assayed beyond your ability and strength of resistance and power to endure, but with the temptation He will [always] also provide the way out (the means of escape to a landing place), that you may be capable and strong and powerful to bear up under it patiently." **1 Corinthians 10:13** (AMP)

Sometimes, when we go through trials and difficulties it's hard to believe that God is with us. We feel he's deserted us, yet this experience reminded me that God is always there, that he is working behind the scenes, watching over us and protecting us. God oversees everything that is happening and he is in control. We may not know it as we don't always see what he is doing. We don't always realise it, but that doesn't change the truth of it and this brings me so much comfort. Paul writes in **2 Corinthians 4:17-18** "17 For our present troubles are small and won't last very long. Yet they produce for us a glory that vastly outweighs them and will last forever! 18 So we don't look at the troubles we can see now; rather, we fix our gaze on things that cannot be seen. For the things we see now will soon be gone, but the things we cannot see will last forever."

God is watching over us all the time, sometimes we can see him working in the situation and at other times when we don't see it, he is working in it just the same.

The Psalmist wrote in **Psalm 121:3-5** "³ He will not let you stumble; the one who watches over you will not slumber. ⁴ Indeed, he who watches over Israel never slumbers or sleeps. ⁵ The Lord himself watches over you! The Lord stands beside you as your protective shade."

These verses apply to us today as much as they did when they were written for the Israelites.

I'm glad God reminded me of these things recently; I just need to keep remembering them, especially when I'm faced with another difficulty or trial. I need to trust and believe in him. Focusing my attention on him, rather than on what is happening around me.

Psalm 20:7 "Some trust in chariots and some in horses, (or in cars or other things) but we trust in the name of the Lord our God." (NIV)

To Think About:

- *What does it mean to you to know that God is always watching over you?*

- *Have you had experience of God working in your life behind the scenes?*

- *Are you able to trust God in the midst of difficulties? What can help you to keep trusting in God?*

Hearing from God

Dear Friend,

Last Sunday morning at church I preached on 'Hearing from God'. Whenever I preach I know that what I'm sharing is as much for me as it is for those who are listening. God really made that very clear to me that very afternoon. I based the message on **1 Samuel 3:1-4:1** and shared how we need to have the same attitude as Samuel, who, when he realised God was speaking to him said "Speak, your servant is listening." **v10**. I shared that if we are really listening to God then we will act on what he says to us no matter how hard it may be.

Jason and I had a decision to make and we had been seeking God for the answer. That afternoon, as we chatted over a cup of tea, Jason shared what he thought God was saying. He said there was a part of him that didn't want to follow through on it, but he couldn't get away from what he felt God was telling him, and God had brought it back to him as I'd been preaching that morning.

To say I was surprised by what Jason thought God was saying to him is an understatement. I was unprepared for what Jason had to say, especially as it didn't make a lot of sense from a human perspective. Because we both see our marriage as a partnership and the decision we needed to make would affect us both, Jason wanted us to come to a joint decision. I agreed that I would take a couple more days to pray and consider what God was saying to us.

That afternoon as I read my daily bible reading God drew my attention to one particular verse which appeared to confirm what he had already said to Jason. The following morning as I had my quiet time with God I was reading an email devotion from "Girlfriends in God". The writer referred to the following verses: **Luke 5:4-5** "When he (Jesus) had finished speaking, he said to Simon, "Put out into deep water, and let down the nets for a catch." ⁵ Simon answered, 'Master, we've worked hard all night and haven't caught anything. But because you say so, I will let down the nets.'" (NIV)

What Jesus was telling Simon Peter to do did not make a lot of sense to him. Fishermen fished at night not during the day. So what Jesus was saying just didn't seem wise or good advice. Peter and John were the fishermen. They were experienced in their jobs; they knew what to do without being told it. Yet, despite having fished all night and catching nothing, despite everything saying to the contrary, they agreed to do what made no sense because they had heard the voice of Jesus and chose to do what he was asking them to do. It meant letting go of what they knew to be right humanly speaking and taking a step of faith.

I believe God was using that example to say to me that Jason had heard correctly, that despite what we knew when we looked at our circumstances, despite our situation seeming to indicate the contrary, we were to listen to God's voice, trust him and be obedient to him by taking that step of faith.

So, even though it was difficult, Jason and I agreed that we were hearing from God and that we were to take the appropriate action of obedience.

I believe it brings God pleasure when any of his children pay attention to his voice and demonstrate their trust in him by their obedience. Our obedience positions us to hear God speak to us again and again and I believe that being in the centre of his will is the best place we can possibly be.

To Think About:

- *Take some time to read the whole of that story in **Luke 5:1-11**. Is there something God wants to say to you through it?*

- *Read **1 Samuel 3:1-4:1**. What can you learn from Samuel's example?*

- *When you hear from God what might stop you from stepping out in faith and obedience?*

Things I've Learnt from My Mother

Dear Friend,

Mother's Day will soon be upon us so I want to concentrate on mothers in this post.

Mothers have such a significant role in the family and we should never underestimate their value and influence. God knows how important the family is and he may perhaps have placed another woman in your life to be a "mother" to you, such as an older sister, an aunt, a grandmother, or someone in your church.

My Mum will never be famous, she will never have her name in a "Who's Who" book, although, more significantly, her name is in God's Book of Life, just as all those who have accepted Christ as their Saviour are named in his book. "They worked along with Clement and the rest of my co-workers, whose names are written in the Book of Life." **Philippians 4:3**. The world may never believe she has contributed anything of significance, but I know there will come the day when God will recognise her for what she has done and will say to her "Well done, my good and faithful servant." **Matthew 25:23** and she will leave a lasting legacy behind her.

I want to share with you some of the things I've learned from my Mum, principles that can be put into practice in every area of life, not just in my role as a Mum myself.

1. Her relationship with God. My Mum taught both my sister and me what it means to have a real relationship with God. She showed us how to put God first in everything. She taught us not just through the things she said but also by her example. It was because of my Mum that I learnt how to pray and have a quiet time with God. She taught me how to have a meaningful relationship with him in every part of my life, not just for a Sunday morning, and how to be a follower of God. "But we know that there is only one God, the Father, who created everything, and we live for him. And there is only one Lord, Jesus Christ, through whom God made everything and through whom we have been given life." **1 Corinthians 8:6**. My relationship with God is the most important relationship I will ever have. As I make my relationship with him a priority, I too can be an example to others of what it means to know and love Christ and what it means to live for him.

2. She made herself available. Growing up I never knew a time when she wasn't there for either my sister or myself. She never gave us the impression that she was too busy for us. She was a great listener. We had her attention the moment we walked in at the end of a day at school. We would sit together over a drink and a biscuit and while we talked about the things on our hearts, she listened. She always made time for us and she made it clear we were valuable to her. We could talk to her about anything and everything, knowing that we were free to do so without being judged or criticised or made to feel small or unimportant. Even now, married and with children of my own, she's at the end of the phone if I need to talk to her and barely a day goes by when we don't chat on the phone. We need to have that kind of listening ear when we are with others and to make ourselves available to them when it's needed. Many people just need someone to talk to, someone who will take the time to listen to them. As we make ourselves available for others they will get a sense of their own worth and value in God's eyes.

3. She demonstrated a servant attitude. Part of God's call on her life was for her to be a mum and she did this wholeheartedly. As she served her family she was also being a servant of God. In **Colossians 3:23-24** we are told "Work willingly at whatever you do, as though you were working for the Lord rather than for people. Remember that the Lord will give you an inheritance as your reward, and that the Master you are serving is Christ." Whatever she did, she did it to the glory of God. I truly believe that my sister and I would not be who we are today without the influence she had (and has) on us.

I never knew her to be selfish in her attitudes or actions. She demonstrated the truth of **Philippians 2:4** "Each of you should look not only to your own interests but also to the interests of others." (NIV). I still remember clearly the hours she spent with me helping me to revise so that I could get a good grade in my GCSE exams. I know too well that she didn't do it for the fun of it, she did it because she loved me and wanted me to reach my potential. I remember as a young mum myself, unable to take care of my own children because of poor health, how she would give up her days to not just be a gran, but be like a second mum to them. This was not a short term thing for her, this went on for years. And there are many more examples I could tell you about her servant heart.

By her example she showed me the importance of relationships and that people matter far more than amassing wealth and possessions. After all, Jesus taught us to "love the LORD your God with all your heart, all your soul, and all your mind.' This is the first and greatest commandment. A second is equally important: 'Love your neighbour as yourself." **Matthew 22:37-39**. In my relationship with others I too can show them I love them by demonstrating a servant attitude.

4. She ensured we had fun even in the tough times. We were not a wealthy family and there were a few occasions as we grew up when we were short of money (although my sister and I never knew about it until much later). I remember one time we were without electricity, but even in that difficult time my Mum stayed positive, kept her trust in God and made sure we had fun. In the evening Mum would light our old fashioned oil lamp, and while my sister and I ate a snack of cheese, apples and sultanas Mum would read to us "The Old Faraway Tree" by Enid Blyton or something similar. To me and my sister this was really special and we actually saw it as Mum giving us a treat. We never saw it as having to go without something because Mum never presented it as such. That time is probably up there in the top ten of my favourite family times! I have learnt from Mum to keep trusting God and to be satisfied in him and to see the difficulties as opportunities to grow my faith in him.

To Think About:

- *What have you learnt from your mother or from one who was a "mother" to you?*

- *Find some way to let her know how much you have appreciated the influence she has had on your life, e.g. send her a card telling her what you learnt from her and what she means to you, take her out to lunch, have a day out together. If she is not around anymore, why not write out a prayer in your journal thanking God for her and for the ways she has been a blessing to you.*

- *To any women readers: Who may God want you to be a "mother" to? Ask God to help you to be the mother he is calling you to be, whether it's to your own children, your grandchildren, a young woman at church, or someone else.*

Practising the Presence of God

Dear Friend,

Today's devotional is a little longer than usual. I found that the more I wrote on this topic, the more I became taken up with it and with God himself. So I suggest either you make yourself your favourite hot drink, settle down on your favourite comfy chair and read, or perhaps read it in two sittings rather than one.

I'm hungry for more of Jesus, for a closer walk with him and to know his presence with me moment by moment. I think this is what the psalmist longed for when he wrote:

Psalm 42:12 "As the deer pants for streams of water, so my soul pants for you, my God. 2 My soul thirsts for God, for the living God. When can I go and meet with God?" (NIV).

It says of Enoch in **Genesis 5:22** that he "walked faithfully with God 300 years" (NIV), the NLT translates it as "lived in close fellowship with God" and the Amplified translates it as "walked [in habitual fellowship] with God". Now there's a great epitaph!

In recent years I've heard people mention Brother Lawrence and his book "The Practice of the Presence of God" which is based on his conversations and letters. I've often wondered what this is about so I decided to download the book on my e-reader and have started to read it. I'm finding it interesting and helpful despite the old-fashioned English. In it Brother Lawrence explains how he has practised the presence of God in his life and maintained a continual conversation with God.

I wonder if the answer to experiencing more of God in my life - having a greater awareness of him with me - is not so much about working hard to have more of him, but is instead about me giving more of myself to him, surrendering my self and my will to him. So, rather than it become a striving after or a duty that I 'should' do as a Christian it flows from my love for him and a desire to worship him in all that I do.

For me, I believe that having a closer walk with God is not about duty but it does include discipline. Too often we can view discipline as a negative thing but I think it is positive. Discipline means to train yourself to do something by controlling your behaviour, and self-control is actually the fruit of the Holy Spirit (**Galatians 5:23**). I think there is a link between discipline and disciple, and as a disciple of Jesus, I am his follower. As I follow him, he teaches me and I learn from him. The more closely I walk with him, following in his path, the more intimately I get to know him. And the more I know him the more I imitate him and the more I become like him.

As I live and move in close fellowship with God I can bring him glory in all that I do. As John the Baptist said "He must increase, but I must decrease. [He must grow more prominent; I must grow less so.]" **John 3:30** (Amp). Life becomes more about God and less about me. "So whether you eat or drink, or whatever you do, do it all for the glory of God." **1 Corinthians 10:31**.

What does it mean practically to practise the presence of God? Well, for me, it's not just when I go to a meeting at church, or meet during the week with other Christians or as I have my quiet time with God. But it's also as ...

... I go about my daily responsibilities and include God in them,

... I have a conversation with him during the things that I do,

... I work on housework, for example, my willing and glad service for my family and for God,

... I ask him for his help in walking close with him,

... I seek his help in the things I'm doing and when they're completed as I give him my thanks for enabling me in what has been done,

... I bake a cake and listen to a bible teacher's message on the radio and ponder what God wants to say to me through it,

... I clean and tidy the living room with Christian music on and the words of a song touch my soul, such as the song which has taken the words from **Psalm 84:10** "Better is one day in your courts than a thousand elsewhere;" (NIV) and which then stays in my heart through the day.

The privilege of praising and worshipping God is a marvellous thing when we realise that God inhabits, or dwells in his people's praises. (**Psalm 22:3, KJV**). He is present when I give him my praise and I wonder if perhaps I am closest to him when I praise him.

I believe the more I "practise the presence of God" as Brother Lawrence put it, the more it will become second nature to me, that it will become as natural as breathing. But, let's be honest here, it will take time. It will take discipline. There will be times when I move away from God's presence. But that doesn't mean I then beat myself up over it, call myself a failure (as is often my way) nor do I give up. Instead, I use it as an opportunity to return to my Heavenly Father, who waits for me with open arms, ready to pour out on me his love, grace and mercy.

I've shared with you some of what I've begun to do, but I don't want to be too prescriptive. After all, it could too easily become all about rules of what must, or should or ought to be and our relationship with God is not about that. Our relationship with God is all about his love and his grace. Each of us, because he has created us as unique individuals, has a unique relationship with him, which means my walk with him will not look like your walk with him.

What I do know is that a close walk with God will enrich my life, and will enrich your life. Not only that, it will enrich the lives of those connected with us - our friends, our family, our neighbours, our community and more.

To Think About:

- *Is God stirring your heart to "practise the presence of God"?*

- *Are you willing to do something about it?*

- *What difference do you think it would make to your life?*

What's so good about Good Friday?

Dear Friend,

One way we learn is through asking questions and I can remember my son, Josh, asking me when he was a young boy, "Why do we call the day Jesus died on the cross Good Friday?" You know, that's a very good question to ask, and by asking it of me he actually made me think seriously about it before responding to him.

Why would anyone name the day we remember someone dying as good? Well, I would think on that day, over 2,000 years ago, the devil thought it must have been a very good day. He must have been rubbing his hands in glee. At last, or so he thought, he was victorious over Jesus. Finally, or so he thought, he had orchestrated the death of his enemy, God's Son. He thought he'd struck God a mortal blow. The religious leaders thought they too had finally got their way by having Jesus put to death on a cross.

Jesus' mother and family, his friends and followers would hardly have thought it a good day as they saw the one they loved tortured beyond recognition and then suffer the humiliating death of a criminal on a cross. Isaiah prophesied that "But many were amazed when they saw him. His face was so disfigured he seemed hardly human, and from his appearance, one would scarcely know he was a man." **Isaiah 52:14**. Can you imagine their pain, grief and despair? In their anguish they had forgotten that Jesus had warned them that this would happen. In **Matthew 16:21** it says "From then on Jesus began to tell his disciples plainly that it was necessary for him to go to Jerusalem, and that he would suffer many terrible things at the hands of the elders, the leading priests, and the teachers of religious law. He would be killed, but on the third day he would be raised from the dead"

Yet, despite appearances, Good Friday was actually a good day. Why? How? What's so good about Good Friday?

The devil believed the day was his victory but he could not have been more wrong. Death was not the end for Jesus because God, in his power, raised him from the dead three days later. Jesus was the victor. Because of Jesus we need have no fear of death, death is not the end for those of us who love God. God has given us eternal life, a life prepared for us to live in heaven with him. "Then, when our dying bodies have been transformed into bodies that will never die, this Scripture will be fulfilled: "Death is swallowed up in victory. 55 O death, where is your victory? O death, where is your sting?" 56 For sin is the sting that results in death, and the law gives sin its power. 57 But thank God! He gives us victory over sin and death through our Lord Jesus Christ." **1 Corinthians 15:54-57**

Through Jesus' death on the cross we have been made righteous with God. God is a holy and just God and therefore the punishment for our sins had to be paid by someone. The only person who could take that punishment was Jesus, he was the only one without sin. "For the wages of sin is death, but the free gift of God is eternal life through Christ Jesus our Lord." **Romans 6:23**. He took all our sins on himself as he was nailed to the cross, the sins of every person who has ever lived and who is yet to live. The sins you and I have already committed and the sins we are yet to commit. God loves us so much that Jesus willingly went to the cross for us so that we might receive God's forgiveness and be welcomed into his family. "In love 5 he predestined us for adoption to sonship through Jesus Christ, in accordance with his pleasure and will— 6 to the

praise of his glorious grace, which he has freely given us in the One he loves. ⁷ In him we have redemption through his blood, the forgiveness of sins, in accordance with the riches of God's grace. ⁸ that he lavished on us with all wisdom and understanding."
Ephesians 1:5-8 (NIV)

These are the reasons why we call the day Jesus died on the cross Good Friday.

To Think About:

- *God's gift to us is one that he freely offers to us all, yet for us to receive it freely he paid the highest price imaginable. Have you accepted his gift? If not, what's holding you back? If you have, how are you using what cost him so dearly to give?*

- *In the days leading up to Easter you might like to read the Easter story. As you do imagine yourself as an eye witness to everything that happens. What do you think God wants to show you as you look once more at Jesus' death and resurrection? Below are the bible passages you could read:*

The Last Supper: Matthew 26:26-29, Mark 14:22-25, Luke 22:14-20. Jesus speaks to his disciples in the Upper Room: John 13-17. Jesus in Gethsemane: Matt 26:36-46, Mark 14:32-42, Luke 22:39-46, John 18:1. Jesus is betrayed and arrested: Matt 26:47-56, Mark 14:43-52, Luke 22:47-53, John 18:2-12. Jesus' trial and Peter's denial of Jesus: Matt 26:57-27:2, 11-31, Mark 14:53-15:20, Luke 22:54-23:25, John 18:13-19:16. Jesus is crucified: Matt 27:31-56, Mark 15:20-41, Luke 23: 26-49, John 19:17-30. Jesus' resurrection: Matt 28:1-10, Mark 16:1-11, Luke 24:1-12, John 20:1-18.

From Dashed Hope to Hope Restored

Dear Friend,

On that first Good Friday, Jesus' followers grieved and mourned not only for Jesus' death but also for the death of their hopes and dreams and for the loss of purpose and meaning to their life. Their hopes were dashed, their dreams deflated and their purpose for living destroyed. All these things had been wrapped up in Jesus and who they thought he was and his purpose for coming. Even though Jesus had explained it to them, they had misunderstood him. They thought he had come to save them from the tyrannical rule of the Romans; they thought he was going to be their military leader. For three days they were grieving the loss of a loved one and they were in despair over all that they had lost. Two disciples on the road to Emmaus said to a stranger (they didn't realise at first he was Jesus in his new resurrection body) "We _had hoped_ he was the Messiah who had come to rescue Israel. This all happened three days ago." **Luke 24:21.** You can read the whole of this account in **Luke 24:13-36.**

Have you ever been in a similar position? Have you experienced the pain of lost hope, lost dreams, lost purpose? Perhaps the hope of a particular job, marriage, starting a family, travelling, serving God? I have been in a similar position to Jesus' followers. I was convinced that it was God's plan for me to go to University to train as a school teacher. I was convinced that his purpose for me was to become a teacher. There was no doubt in my mind that this was the direction my life was going.

However, despite completing my teaching degree, despite filling in numerous application forms and attending interviews, a full-time teaching job did not open up for me. Then, not long after, I became ill with M.E and due to poor health was not able to work in any kind of job. How could this be? How could this happen? I was sure it had been God's plan for me to work as a full-time teacher, but I never saw this fulfilled. My hopes and dreams were dashed. They died because they came to nothing.

Going back to that first Good Friday, it was not the end and Jesus' followers had Easter Sunday. When God raised Jesus to new life on that Sunday, Jesus brought with him hope restored, dreams revised, his plan and purpose revealed. His followers finally understood what God's plan had been all along. Yes, Jesus had come to earth to save them but not in the way they had dreamed. He had come to save all people from the power of sin, to redeem us and restore us to a loving relationship with our Heavenly Father.

They now understood what Jesus' purpose was and the part that they had (and now we have) to play in God's plan. *Jesus came and told his disciples, 'I have been given all authority in heaven and on earth. 19 Therefore, go and make disciples of all the nations, baptizing them in the name of the Father and the Son and the Holy Spirit. 20 Teach these new disciples to obey all the commands I have given you. And be sure of this: I am with you always, even to the end of the age.'"* **Matthew 28:18-20.** It was so much better than what they had expected and hoped for and they saw this now. They had to go through Good Friday to get to Easter Sunday.

I still believe that it was God's plan all along for me to attend university and gain a teacher training degree. However, at the time I had misunderstood why it was God's plan. It became much clearer later, that all the experiences in those years were to prepare me for when I taught and led in Sunday School, to prepare me to teach women in small groups and for preaching and teaching in a church setting. I had learnt many skills, including how to communicate with others, how to teach, how to study and also how to lean on God. I needed to go through my own Good Friday to come through to the other side, Easter Sunday, where hope was restored, dreams revised and God's purpose for me revealed. The things God had planned for me are so much better than what I had originally supposed. In **Ephesians 3:20** Paul writes "Now to Him Who, by (in consequence of) the [action of His] power that is at work within us, is able to [carry out His purpose and] do superabundantly, far over and above all that we [dare] ask or think [infinitely beyond our highest prayers, desires, thoughts, hopes, or dreams]—" (AMP)

Perhaps you have come through the other side and you can look back and see the things God had planned for you and you are living in the light of his hope and his purpose for you. Perhaps he has given you a new dream to replace the original one you had. Perhaps you can see now how much better life is, how it is so much more than you had hoped for.

But perhaps some of you are still in Good Friday, and you still need the time to mourn and grieve for the things you have lost. That's ok, we need to feel what we are feeling, to recognise the emotions we are experiencing. But, let me encourage you, hold onto hope because although it may be Friday, Sunday is coming! Hallelujah!

Psalm 30:5b "Weeping may last through the night, but joy comes with the morning."

To Think About:

- *Do you have any hopes, dreams, plans that have died?*

- *Has God breathed new life or restores or revealed to you a new purpose, a new hope, a new dream?*

- *Are you living in Easter Sunday? How can you partner with him to see his hopes and dreams and plans fulfilled in you?*

Learning to Forgive Ourselves

Dear Friend,

Forgiving others for what they have done against us is not easy, but forgiving ourselves for our own sins and failings can be just as hard. To be honest, it's something I really struggle with.

I know the truth that *"If we confess our sins to him, he is faithful and just to forgive us our sins and to cleanse us from all wickedness."* **1 John 1:9.** I know that the moment I turn to God, confess my sins to him, he forgives me totally and completely. Yet I still have a hard time forgiving myself.

I think perhaps it's partly because of the person I am that I sometimes find it hard to forgive myself. I'm a perfectionist, which I used to think was a positive quality, but over the past years God has been teaching me differently (but that's a story for another time.) I expect to get things right all the time, to be perfect, and so when I'm not, I'm very hard on myself and unforgiving.

Then, when I think I've learned to forgive myself and accept God's forgiveness, along comes Satan. He's so clever. He knows me well, he knows where I'm weakest, he knows which buttons to press, and he works on those feelings of guilt I have as a mum. He brings to mind the times I've got it wrong in my parenting. He whispers lies in my ear that I have failed in the past as a mother, that the children have suffered because of my mistakes, that I am just no good. The reality is that they are lies he tells me because the Bible tells us he's the father of lies and his intention is to cause us pain and misery and he wants to take away everything that we have in Christ Jesus.

Yet I listen to those lies, I take them as truth, I feel weighed down by guilt and I struggle once again to forgive myself.

So how do we move forward? How do we learn to forgive ourselves? To let go of the unforgiveness and feelings of guilt that weigh us down?

1. **We need to <u>recognise</u> the devil's lies and choose not to listen to them.**

2. **Then we need to <u>replace</u> them with God's truth.**

To do that, we need to know God's truth. Such as **1 John 1:9** and "So now there is no condemnation for those who belong to Christ Jesus." **Romans 8:1.** You see, it's not God who reminds us of our past forgiven sins: He chooses to remember our sins no more and we need to do the same. The devil is the one who takes great joy in reminding us of our sins as he seeks to destroy the hope, peace and joy we have in Christ Jesus. This is what God does with our sins. "He has removed our sins as far from us as the east is from the west." **Psalm 103:12**

"Where is another God like you, who pardons the guilt of the remnant, overlooking the sins of his special people? You will not stay angry with your people forever, because you delight in showing unfailing love. Once again you will have compassion on us. You will trample our sins under your feet and throw them into the depths of the ocean!" **Micah 7:18-19**

I really like the example Corrie Ten Boom (a survivor of a World War 2 concentration camp) gives: "When we confess our sins God casts them into the deepest ocean, gone forever. I believe God then places a sign out there that says, 'NO FISHING ALLOWED.'"

3. Remember the truth of God's Word.

Memorise it, write these verses and others like them on small pieces of card so that you can keep them with you, put the cards in your wallet, or on the fridge, or by your bed or on the mirror in your bathroom, anywhere you can see them regularly and read them. Then when the guilt returns, when you're reminded of your past sins and mistakes and when you recognise the whispers of the devil in your ear, you can speak out these truths in faith. Remember, you have God's Holy Spirit within you, he's always with you. Ask him to help you to have the faith to believe the truth and to live in the light of that truth, not bound up, disabled or held down by lies.

To Think About:

- *Is there any past sin in your life which you are not able to forgive yourself for?*

- *Do you believe the truth that God has forgiven you of all your sins? Have you accepted the forgiveness he offers?*

- *Practise the three points mentioned above.*

God is Faithful

Dear Friend,

When God commanded Noah to build the ark, Noah obeyed. He did everything that God commanded him to do. You can read the account of Noah in **Genesis Chapters 6-9**.

Noah, his wife, his three sons and their wives along with the animals who entered the ark were kept safe and protected. They were in the ark for nearly a whole year. Can you imagine what it must have been like to have spent almost a year in the ark? The noise and smell from the animals, not being free to wander outside and smell the fresh air - the waiting and the patience needed to wait.

I wonder if, after all those months, Noah experienced times of doubt. Had God forgotten him? Did God care about him at all? Had he really heard from God in the first place? Would he spend the rest of his life confined to the ark?

I know for myself there are times when I wonder if God has forgotten about me. Perhaps you've been there too - a situation where it feels that God has forgotten you, where he doesn't seem to be acting on your behalf. It may be that some time ago you felt God saying something to you, but he hasn't yet fulfilled his word. The situation hasn't changed, your health hasn't improved as you thought it would, your marriage is falling apart, the job promotion you thought would be yours has gone to another colleague, the rift in your relationship with your children is still there, God hasn't provided you with a spouse, your dreams of a new role in ministry haven't been fulfilled even though you believed God was leading you in that direction. Whatever the situation is for you, you begin to wonder if God really cares as you thought he did, there seems no way out, and you even begin to wonder if you really did hear from God in the first place.

I find so much encouragement in the verse *"But God remembered Noah..."* **Genesis 8:1**. God isn't like us. Sometimes Jason will ask me to do something for him, which I agree to do, but evening comes and I realise I've forgotten to do what he's asked, or it may be a friend's birthday and I'll mean to send a card in the post, I remember too late and need to send a belated one. Or I intend to do something and get distracted by something else. I am so glad that God isn't like that – he never forgets, is never late and never gets distracted.

When it says *"But God remembered Noah..."* what it really means is that now was the time for God to act on someone's - in this case - Noah's, behalf. God remembered Noah; he kept him safe during the flood and brought him out of the ark to experience the blessing God had planned for him – a new life.

Be encouraged, that whatever your circumstances are right now God has not forgotten you, he has not been distracted by another matter, he's not been side-tracked and he is not late! At the right time, and by the way, the right time is in his time, he will "remember" you, he will act on your behalf.

The hard part for us is waiting and trusting in God for his timing. I'm sure Noah would have liked to have left the ark earlier than he did, but that would most likely have ended in disaster because the time wouldn't have been right. Only God knew when the right time was, when the best time was, and when that came, he acted. We often wish God would act more quickly, but when he doesn't we need to trust him that he does know best and when the time comes he does promise to act.

Is God Calling You to Something New?

Dear Friend,

When you sense that God may be calling you to something new, to take a step of faith, you can experience a variety of emotions. On the one hand there may be excitement as you think about the plan God has for your life and where he is leading you. On the other hand, you may be anxious about facing the unknown and what he is asking you to do. Or perhaps stubbornly you decide to dig in your heels because you don't want the change. You may be wondering why he is calling you to do something different when you are satisfied with life as it is, when you already consider yourself productive in your relationships, home, work, ministry at church etc. To leave all that behind may not make a lot of sense to you.

I wonder what emotions Abram experienced when he heard God's call on his life. Abram was from a prominent family, his ancestry could be traced all the way back to Seth, Adam and Eve's son. His was a wealthy family with many possessions and servants. Then in **Genesis 12:1** he receives this call from God: "The LORD had said to Abram, "Leave your native country, your relatives, and your father's family, and go to the land that I will show you."

God's call to him was to leave and follow his direction; there was no real explanation, just the command to go somewhere new. God was calling Abram to leave all that he knew – his people and his way of living. He was calling Abram to move from his place of security, comfort and position and on into the unknown. Abram had no idea where God was calling him to; God had not revealed that part of his plan yet. It took incredible faith on Abram's part, to trust and be obedient to God's word. We read in **Hebrews 11:8** *"It was by faith that Abraham obeyed when God called him to leave home and go to another land that God would give him as his inheritance. He went without knowing where he was going."*

It can be far from easy for us to move out of our comfort zone, out of what is familiar to us and to follow God's direction, especially when we don't know where that might be. Although God has the whole plan mapped out, he often takes us just one step at a time, asking us to put our trust in him, depend on him and him alone. Taking that step of faith is scary, we often prefer to stay where we are. After all, we had it all figured out, we knew exactly where our life was heading, what was just around the corner, or so we thought. We were settled and comfortable. And then God steps in and tells us he's got something new for us, a new direction to take.

Abram, from a human point of view, had pretty much all he needed: things were good for him, there was no reason to change and move on until God stepped in suddenly and directed him to something new. I don't know how those left behind felt about him leaving them, maybe they didn't understand, maybe they thought he'd got it wrong, but none of this deterred Abram from stepping out as God told him to.

In faith Abram stepped out and was obedient to God and as we read through the Bible we learn just how much God did for and through this man of faith. If Abram had chosen to stay where he was, to disobey God's call, he would have missed out on all that God had planned for him; he would not have known the blessings God had in store for him.

It's the same with us. If we are disobedient to God's call on our life we miss out on all the wonderful things God has planned for us, we will miss out on the incredible life that is waiting for us the moment we say yes to him. When we say yes to him and step out in faith and obedience, God will do amazing things for and through us.

The notes in my NLT Parallel Study Bible read "God may be trying to lead you to a place of greater service and usefulness for him." I also read that you and I shouldn't let what we have now, "the comfort and security of your present position make you miss God's plan for you."

To Think About:

- *In what area of your life do you sense God is leading you into something new? In your relationships? Your home? Your work? Your church ministry?*

- *Do you need to do what Abram did and leave or let go of something in order to follow God's call and do that new thing he has planned for you?*

- *Will you step out in faith and be obedient to God?*

You Are God's Masterpiece!

Dear Friend,

Do you see yourself as God sees you? As his masterpiece? What makes something a masterpiece, a real work of art? Not the object itself, but the master artist who created it and designed it. For example, Van Gogh's pieces of art were not masterpieces in themselves; they were masterpieces because of the one who created them.

Therefore, I'm not a masterpiece because of anything I do or have achieved but I am one because I've been created by GOD - THE MASTER DESIGNER.

"For we are God's masterpiece. He has created us anew in Christ Jesus, so we can do the good things he planned for us long ago."
Ephesians 2:10

Don't you just love that! I know I do. You and I are God's masterpiece! How amazing is that! (I know there are several exclamation marks in this short paragraph, but it's something I want to exclaim, it thrills me to the depth of my very being.) You may want to spend some time allowing the words of that verse to nourish your soul, to heal past hurts from the lies people have said about you and to you. Let those words soak in and bring you comfort and encouragement.

Over the years I've struggled with a poor self-image. Growing up I never felt as beautiful as my peers. I wasn't popular, I believed people liked my sister far more than they liked me. I wasn't clever, I had to work incredibly hard to get decent grades and I was painfully shy, barely able to open my mouth, believing that I didn't really have anything to say that was worth listening to. I'm not telling you these things to make you feel sorry for me; I'm sharing them to say that I'm learning now to see myself as God sees me – as his masterpiece, as precious to him, someone who is of worth. Maybe you can relate to what I'm sharing. It all comes down to changing the way we think and learning to believe what God says about us and not holding on to what others or even we ourselves have said in the past.

I confess, even now I sometimes look at others and wish I were more like them - more talkative, or had a particular gift they had. But God keeps reminding me that when I think like that, I am, in essence, complaining to him, telling him he got it wrong with me, that he's made a mistake. When the truth is, God never makes mistakes, he is THE MASTER DESIGNER and he created me on purpose, just as I am, for a purpose. This is the truth that we all need to grab hold of. I may not be a great talker, but God has created me to be a good listener. You may be a great talker and God can use that ability to make people feel welcomed, comfortable and at ease around you. God has given me spiritual gifts, and he has given you different ones. They are suited to the person he has created you and me to be.

When we know and believe this – that he has created us for a purpose, we can begin to live in that purpose and enjoy it as we do so. He planned it out even before we were born.

Read how the Amplified Bible translates **Ephesians 2:10** "For we are God's [own] handiwork (His workmanship), recreated in Christ Jesus, [born anew] that we may do those good works which God predestined (planned beforehand) for us [taking paths which He prepared ahead of time], that we should walk in them [living the good life which He prearranged and made ready for us to live]."

Do you realise God only wants the best for us? Do the words of that verse fill you with hope and excitement? It does me.

To Think About:

- *Do you see yourself as God sees you? If you don't, ask him to help you believe the truth of who you are in Christ – loved, valuable, and someone worth dying for.*

- *Do you believe God created you on purpose and for a purpose?*

- *What is your God-given purpose? If you don't yet know what your purpose is, spend time alone with God asking him to make it clear to you.*

- *Ask God to show you how he wants you to live out your purpose every day.*

God Calls You for a Purpose

Dear Friend,

The God who created the world and everything in it desires to have a relationship with you and me. Do you know that he knows you by name? How incredible is that? There are around seven billion people on this earth and God knows you by name. God is calling us into a relationship with him.

Isaiah 43:1 says *"But now, O Jacob, listen to the Lord who created you. O Israel, the one who formed you says, "Do not be afraid, for I have ransomed you. I have called you by name; you are mine."*

God created us first and foremost for a relationship with him; a relationship with him is the most fulfilling one we can ever experience. God knows us better than we know ourselves and he loves us unconditionally. He is the source of all that we need; a relationship with him brings us peace, hope, joy, love and fulfilment. No other relationship can meet all our needs and if we look to others to supply them we will end up feeling disappointed. In the past I have looked to others to do this, I've looked to them for security, for self-worth, for approval; etc., but this has only led to disappointment for me as they have never been able to measure up (who could possibly measure up to God?); and for them, the pressure or burden has just been too great, because they were never created to be the ones to meet my every need. I am learning to look to God as the source of all I need. I say learning, rather than learnt, as I still sometimes fall back into the mistake of looking to others. We need one another but our primary relationship is with

God. Our relationships with others will flow out of our relationship with God.

Not only does God call us to a relationship with him, he also calls us for a purpose. When we are secure in our relationship with him, when he is first in our lives, then we can trust in his purpose for us. God has a plan for your life that only you can fulfil. You will experience such joy, pleasure and peace when you live out God's plan for you. You will know the assurance of doing what God has called you to do. It has brought me so much joy and peace doing what he's called me to and also released me from having to do things which he has not called me to do. I get excited when I'm living out God's purpose for me, knowing that this is what I was made for.

God's calling on your life doesn't change; however, the expression of that calling may change in a new season. For example, I believe God has called me to teach and share the truths of his Word. I believe he has been preparing me for this all my life. The expression of this calling has changed over time from teaching in small groups, to being a part of our church's preaching team, to sharing God's Word in my blog.

God called Jeremiah to a relationship with him and to serve him: "The LORD gave me this message: 'I knew you before I formed you in your mother's womb. Before you were born I set you apart and appointed you as my prophet to the nations.'" **Jeremiah 1:4-5**

In Jill Briscoe's book "Faith Enough to Finish" she writes that when God calls you to do something he will equip you for it. On your own it may seem impossible, but because God equips you it is possible. Your confidence is one that is found in him, it is not self-confidence.

To Think About:

- *Is there any relationship in your life that takes God's place?*

- *Do you need to rearrange the relationships in your life so that God takes priority?*

- *Spend some time considering the purpose God has called you to.*

- *Do you rely on the Holy Spirit's anointing to equip you for that purpose?*

We Need One Another

Dear Friend,

"Dear friends, I am not writing a new commandment for you; rather it is an old one you have had from the very beginning. This old commandment—to love one another—is the same message you heard before. 8 Yet it is also new. Jesus lived the truth of this commandment, and you also are living it." **1 John 2:7-8**

We need one another if we are to walk the Christian life as God intended.

I'm an introvert and reserved by nature. I'm happy with my own company – I just need a good book to read and a decaffeinated skinny latte with a shot of caramel and I'm well away! However, I also know how important it is to surround myself with good Christian friends so that I can really flourish as a Christian.

I've had people say to me that they don't need to come to church to live their Christian life. But that's not what my Bible teaches. Coming to church won't make you a Christian, but we all need to be connected; we can't live the Christian life on our own, and we are definitely better together. There are so many instances in the bible where we are taught to connect with each other. That doesn't mean we will have a deep, close relationship with everyone, but we all need a group of people around us with whom we can share honestly and openly, where we can give and receive encouragement, comfort, support, as well as advice, a listening ear and people who are willing to point out where perhaps we have gone off course and need to re-focus and get back on track.

Take a look at some of the things the Bible teaches us to do for "one another":

- Love one another: Romans 13:8, Philippians 2:2, 1 Thessalonians 4:9, 1 John 3:11
- Serve one another: Galatians 5:13, I Peter 4:10
- Motivate one another to acts of love and good works: Hebrews 10:24
- Don't judge one another: Romans 14:13 (NIV)
- Accept one another: Romans 15:7
- Encourage one another: Hebrews 10:25, 1 Thessalonians 5:11 (NIV)
- Be kind and compassionate to one another: Ephesians 4:32 (NIV)
- Forgive one another: Ephesians 4:32
- Teach and admonish one another: Colossians 3:16 (NIV)
- Fellowship with one another: 1 John 1:7 (NIV)
- Bear one another's burdens: Galatians 6:2 (NKJV)
- Comfort one another: 1 Thessalonians 5:11 (NKJV)

These seem to me to be a good description of what friendship should be. They are some great qualities to have in my own life and to look for in a friend. God has blessed me with some really good friends. My life would be so much poorer without them in it. We make time for each other and we meet up over coffee and cake or a meal and share about ourselves and our families, there are times when we pray together, and there are also times when we just hang out together and have fun. We look out for each other, send each other an encouraging text or email, or chat on the phone. These relationships mean so much to me and they play an important part in my Christian journey and living for Christ.

I also meet regularly with a fantastic group of mums who love the Lord Jesus as I do. These mums have also become my good friends. In fact, we met just this last Wednesday morning. They are my loved sisters in Christ and we have such a blessed time together. We share together from the heart, our joys and our heartaches, we laugh together, cry together and we pray together. We learn from each other and are a source of comfort, support and encouragement to each other. Studying God's Word together is also a big part of our gatherings. I love to hear what each one is learning from God as they seek to tune themselves to hear his voice as they read their bible. In this way we are learning and growing together. I'm like a proud mum when I see how much they are growing and becoming more like Christ.

I would like to encourage you to make sure you too have some significant friends in your life - people who love Jesus just as you do and have the same aims as you do. These friendships shouldn't be characterised by one of you doing all the receiving and one doing all the giving; they should be ones in which both are blessed and benefit from it.

If you want to know more about being a friend you could do no better than to look at the life of Jesus.

To Think About:

- *What does being a good friend mean to you?*

- *What could you do to celebrate the friendship you have with a good friend?*

- *Is there a particular person you feel God drawing you to befriend? What will you do about it?*

- *Perhaps now is the time to re-evaluate your friendships. Is there one that needs to be nurtured? Or is there one God is saying you need to let go of because it's not a healthy relationship.*

God - Our Heavenly Father

Dear Friend,

With Father's Day approaching, I find that my thoughts are turning to God as my Heavenly Father.

I have been so blessed in growing up with a Dad who loves me unconditionally, who instructed and guided me, who gave advice and disciplined me when needed. He isn't a perfect Dad, no man is, but under God, he is the best Dad he could be and he has provided me with a good example of what God as my Heavenly Father is like. I would not be the woman of faith today without my Dad.

God loves us unconditionally and desires us to know him as our Father. He is always there for us, he instructs, teaches and guides and disciplines us too. As our Father he wants the best for us and has a wonderful inheritance waiting for us to claim.

"See how very much our Father loves us, for he calls us his children, and that is what we are!" **1 John 3:1**

When we were growing up, my Dad used a phrase on various occasions with my sister and me. He would say "Let's walk and talk."

Whenever my sister or I were upset for whatever reason – a difficult day at school, issues with boyfriends, failing a driving test – my Dad would say "Let's walk and talk". He and I (or my sister) would bundle our dogs (Silas and Barney named after Paul's travelling companions in the Bible, Silas and Barnabas, my Dad also being named Paul) in the car and Dad would drive to Ashdown Forest where we would walk and Dad would listen to my woes, share my heartache, talk with me and make me feel better. The situation I faced may not always have changed but I was helped just by being able to share it, to put it into perspective, to know that I had a Dad who cared and was on my side. What Dad was doing was giving me his undivided attention: there was no chance of our being interrupted by a phone call or the doorbell ringing, or being distracted by other responsibilities. While we walked he was devoting his time and attention to me, and I knew, for the time allotted to that walk, that no-one else and nothing else mattered to him like I did.

I didn't realise it at the time, but he was modelling the Father heart of God, and the relationship God wants with each of his children. Throughout the bible we have examples of God walking with his children, one such example being *"Enoch lived 365 years, walking in close fellowship with God."* **Genesis 5:23-24**

What a privilege we have to "walk and talk" with God our Father. He is waiting for us to approach him, to ask him to walk beside us. He is always available to give us his undivided attention, and he wants to spend time with us. We can come to him at any time, knowing he loves and cares for us. We can share with him whatever is on our minds, both our heartaches and our joys. He helps us to re-focus, to regain our perspective and give us the strength to face whatever comes our way.

I just love the idea of living a life in which I am walking in close fellowship with God. There is nowhere else I would rather be than walking step by step with my loving Heavenly Father and in close communication with him.

To Think About:

- *Do you know God as your Father? If not ask him to reveal himself to you as your Heavenly Father.*

- *Is there something, a burden, a worry, a concern, a heartache, that you need to take before God and "walk and talk" with him?*

- *Have you heard God's call to "walk and talk" with him? What does that mean to you?*

Times of Celebration

Dear Friend,

There is much about praising God and celebrating in the Bible. I believe God wants us to be a people who celebrate and rejoice. **Psalm 145** is a great Psalm about celebrating and praising God. **Verse 7** reads "They celebrate your abundant goodness and joyfully sing of your righteousness." (NIV)

The month of June in our home is a great month for celebrating. As I thought about writing this I considered all of the celebrations that happen for my family in June, and how it's not just about enjoying the celebrations, but recognising that God has provided me with the reason to celebrate and therefore he is worthy of my praise and thanksgiving for all he has given me.

Recently, it was Father's Day – it was a day for my family to celebrate Jason as the father of our children. God has created him to be a role model for our children, to show them what it means to be a man of God. He is an example for Josh to copy and shows Jess the kind of man she should look for when the time comes for her to consider boyfriends (which I know will come all too soon) and the kind of man she should marry. I praise and thank God that Jason is a good Dad.

On 18th June Jess had her twelfth birthday – I believe that children are a gift from God and her birthday is an opportunity to celebrate this truth. "Children are a gift from the LORD; they are a reward from him." **Psalm 127:3**. She is growing into a beautiful young lady.

I know God has good plans and a purpose for her (just as he does for Josh). I celebrate that he has helped me to be her mum for the past twelve years and he will continue to do so. I'm so thankful to know that God is with her, and that he loves her. I look forward to watching as her life unfolds.

On 24th June it will be our eighteenth anniversary – how time flies! An anniversary is an opportunity to celebrate that God has been with us throughout our marriage so far and he has blessed us so much. Of course, there have been ups and downs over the years but God has kept us as we've made him a priority in our own lives and in our marriage. Jason is a wonderful husband, who has had to cope with a lot. For most of our marriage he has had to live with my long-term illness, and I know that's not been easy for him. But he has certainly demonstrated his vow "to love me in sickness..." Jason and I complement each other and I love partnering with him. I'm so thankful to God for bringing him into my life.

On the 30th it will be Jason's birthday (a special one I might add, but you won't get out of me which one!) – the four of us are looking forward to celebrating his 40th (oops!!) in Paris, although I can't say I'm looking forward to leaving home at 4am! I praise and thank God for the man Jason is, I've had my prayers answered as I've seen him grow and mature spiritually. I'm so proud of him as I see him live out God's great plan and purpose for him, and I'm sure God's got even more in store for him.

These are just some of the times when celebrating and rejoices comes easily, but there are also times when it's not so easy to rejoice. We all go through those difficult times, although each one is unique to the individual facing them. There are times for me when I have to choose to praise God and choose to be joyful. When it's a matter of the will and not about the way that I'm feeling. I find the verse in Philippians that Paul wrote while he was in prison, helpful: *"Rejoice in the Lord always. I will say it again: Rejoice!"*

Philippians 4:4. You see, it's not about rejoicing in our circumstances but it's all about rejoicing in the Lord – in who he is and what he means to us. We can do this with the aid of the Holy Spirit who gives us his joy.

To Think About:

- *What is there today that you can give thanks and praise to God for?*

- *Plan to enjoy a celebration with friends and/or family. There doesn't even need to be a specific reason it could be just to enjoy one another's company.*

- *Are you finding it hard at this time to be joyful? Why not take it to the Lord and ask him for help. You may not be able to rejoice right now but hold onto the promise that there will come a time when you can. The Psalmist wrote in* **Psalm 30:5** *"weeping may stay for the night, but rejoicing comes in the morning."* (NIV)

What Is Your Heart's Desire?

Dear Friend,

A few mornings back I was praying and talking over with God what I'm passionate about - my hopes and longings, those which have not yet been fulfilled in my life. I was asking him that if these longings, or desires are really from him, as I believe they are, that he would fulfil them in my life. I also prayed that he would help me to be patient for his timing, and asked him for the wisdom to know when I need to take action and when I need to just wait for him to open the way.

Then later that morning I was reading **Psalm 37** and the following verse particularly struck me:

"Take delight in the LORD, and he will give you your heart's desires." **Psalm 37:4**

What a wonderful promise God makes to give us the desires of our heart. Of course, there is also the premise in that verse that we are firstly to take delight in God. We can't expect God to give us our hopes, dreams and desires if we're choosing to live for ourselves and going our own way.

What does it mean to delight in God? I think it's about enjoying being in God's presence. It's about really knowing God and knowing his love for me and in turn loving him. How do I get to know and love him more? By spending time in his presence.

I take great delight in being with Jason and my children. It's not necessarily about doing something with them, but it is about being together, enjoying each other's company. It's the same with me and God.

I think there's also some great advice in the following verses from Psalm 37 which are applicable to taking delight in God and God giving us our heart's desires:

1.   **Commit everything you do to the Lord. v5** This is about committing myself to God – all that I am, my will, my desires, my ambitions, giving him my all, surrendering to him and his will and what he wants for me.

2.   **Trust him, and he will help you. v5** When I commit myself to God and trust him for everything then I have nothing to fear or worry about as I know he is in control of my life. I can have trust in him and his Word because he is always faithful. I know that I can trust him with my whole being, including my dreams and ambitions. I have confidence that he is my help and my guide. The one who shows me the way forward and which path to take.

3.   **Be still in the presence of the Lord, v7**. Taking delight in God is also about being still in his presence, taking the time to listen to him and learn what his plans and hopes for my life are.

4.   **Wait patiently for him to act. v7** During this time I need to wait for God to act and waiting patiently is not easy, at least I don't find it easy! God knows that it's good for me to wait patiently. Only he knows when the right time to act is. I can so easily get carried away with what I would like to happen, that I can act too soon. Waiting on God stops me from acting too soon and also prepares me for when the time is right. Waiting gives me time to align my desires with God's desires. It gives God opportunity to show me where I may have got it wrong and point me in the right

direction. Waiting on God can also deepen my confidence and dependence in God's Word and his will so that I can hold firm to the desires that God places in my heart.

To Think About:

- *What is the desire of your heart?*

- *Which of the four points mentioned above to do you believe God is particularly drawing your attention to?*

- *What will you do about it?*

El-Roi - The God Who Sees Me

Dear Friend,

I've been reading the account of Hagar in **Genesis 16**.

Here was a woman completely broken by her circumstances. As Sarah's servant she was told to sleep with Abraham so that she could conceive a child on Sarah's behalf. When Sarah learns that Hagar is pregnant, she becomes jealous. She takes her jealousy out on Hagar by mistreating and abusing her. With no control over her situation, Hagar thinks her only option is to run away, rather than face it.

At this point, the lowest point in her life so far, she has an encounter with the Living God. At the time when she feels completely on her own, deserted by everyone, with no-one on her side, God makes his presence known. He makes it clear to her that he has heard her distress and he cares about her.

"And the angel also said, "You are now pregnant and will give birth to a son. You are to name him Ishmael (which means 'God hears'), for the LORD has heard your cry of distress." **Genesis 16:11**

This will be a powerful reminder to her for the rest of her life that God hears her, that he is on her side, that he has not deserted her.

Having experienced the blessing of a relationship with God she calls him El-Roi (The God who sees me).

"Thereafter, Hagar used another name to refer to the LORD, who had spoken to her. She said, 'You are the God who sees me.'"
Genesis 16:13

What a comfort and encouragement that must have been to Hagar. God saw who she was and saw who she would be. Someone who loved her, who didn't consider her a nobody or think she was insignificant.

God then gave her the strength to face the situation, to return and submit to Sarah. Hagar was able to do this because she knew God was with her, close enough to see and hear what was happening in her life.

I find much encouragement from Hagar's experience. It's so reassuring to know that when I'm struggling with a situation, when things are hard, when I feel like I'm on my own and that no one understands, that when I cry out to God in my distress he hears me because he cares about me, he sees, he notices what I'm going through. Let's choose to believe the truth of God's Word rather than believe the lies that say it's not worth calling out to God because he's not listening, he doesn't care and doesn't think we're worth noticing.

It's incredible to know that the Almighty God is the God who sees me - wow! He sees just who I am and who I will be. In those times when I feel ignored, unnoticed and unseen by those around me, it's so good to remember that God sees me as someone who is worthy of his notice because he created me and loves me.

God hears and sees and wants to be involved in every detail of my life and yours. Knowing that he hears and sees us gives us the confidence to face anything, because we know that he is with us and will give us the grace to endure.

Writing about the privilege of having such a relationship with God has caused me to consider some things. I know that God hears and sees me, but how much do I really hear and see God? How much of my attention do I give to him so that I can hear from him? Do I take the time to see and notice him working in my life? Are my eyes focused on him?

To Think About:

- *What encouragement and comfort do you receive from knowing God hears and sees you?*

- *Are you in a situation right now where you need to cry out to God and receive his help, strength and grace?*

- *Is there someone you know who would also be blessed by hearing your story of how God hears and sees?*

God Calls You and God Chooses You

Dear Friend,

I find so much encouragement in the following verses:

Isaiah 41:9-10 "I took you from the ends of the earth from its farthest corners I called you. I said, 'You are my servant'; I have chosen you and have not rejected you. So do not fear, for I am with you; do not be dismayed, for I am your God. I will strengthen you and help you; I will uphold you with my righteous right hand."

God is calling each one of us into a relationship with him (v9). More than anything he wants us to enjoy a relationship with him. Not only does he call us to him, he also places a call on our lives – something he has created you for that only you can do. I've known his call on my life for some years now and it brings me so much enjoyment and fulfilment. Having said that, I don't always find it easy and sometimes I get discouraged (v10a), sometimes I succumb to negative feelings and thoughts. I can begin to compare myself with others and think they're so much better at their calling than I am.

I looked in my journal and God gave me these verses back in the summer of 2007. They were a source of great encouragement then, and as I meditate on them again as I write this, they are once more an encouragement to me.

God says he's with me and he's my God. Therefore, I don't need to be afraid or discouraged (v10a). Then come his wonderful promises: Vicki, I called you, and I called you to work with me, not to go it alone, in your own strength, believe what I say, believe me, I promise to give you strength, I promise to help you and I promise to hold you up (v10b). Wow! How much do I need to hear and hold onto that when I start to feel afraid or discouraged. I'm guessing that I'm not very different from you, and that you too need to hold onto the promises of God as much as I do.

Now for another truth – God has chosen me, he has chosen you. I need that reminder sometimes, that God considers me someone who is special, worth while, and loveable and he chooses me. He didn't need to, he could have decided not to, but instead he did choose me. Please pause for a moment as you read this, allow the truth to soak into your inner being, to soothe your soul, to bless you – God chose you!

I used to dread P.E lessons at school (I was no athlete! One bonus of having my appendix out at secondary school meant there was a legitimate reason for having a few weeks of not being allowed to take part in P.E.) I especially disliked it when we were to be separated into two teams. The captains were always the girls who excelled in sports and were also popular. I would stand waiting to be chosen, feeling more and more uncomfortable, knowing that I would be last or one of the last to be picked. If you had a similar experience growing up you'll know how awful it was, how terrible it made you feel, how it appeared to confirm that others' opinions of you were similar to the low opinion you held of yourself.

But thank God that it's not like that with him. He looks at me, and when he looks at me he sees Jesus, the one who has made me righteous. He sees someone valuable, worth loving, with gifts and abilities. He looks me in the eye, smiles and says "I choose you! I pick you for my team!" Not because he has to, or he's run out of people to ask, or because he feels sorry for me, but because he wants to, because he loves me. He says the same to you too. And hearing that floods my being with warmth, peace and hope. I stand a little taller, my head held up with the assurance that the Almighty God has chosen me and I begin to see myself as God sees me.

To Think About:

- *Take some time to meditate on these verses, and as you do, ask God what he wants you to hear from him.*

- *You may have experienced rejection in the past which has had an impact on how you see yourself. How does it make you feel knowing that God has chosen you?*

- *Have you heard God's call on your life? What will you do about it? What do you think is the next step he wants you to take?*

In God's Hands a "Cracked Pot" Can be Useful

Dear Friend,

I came across 'The Story of a Cracked Pot' a few weeks back and it greatly encouraged me. Have a read:

A water bearer in India had two large pots, one hung on each end of a pole, which she carried across her neck.

One of the pots had a crack in it. While the other pot was perfect, and always delivered a full portion of water at the end of the long walk from the stream to the mistress's house, the cracked pot arrived only half full.

For a full two years this went on daily, with the bearer delivering only one and a half pots full of water to her master's house.

The perfect pot was proud of its accomplishments, perfect to the end for which it was made. But the poor cracked pot was ashamed of its own imperfection, and miserable that it was able to accomplish only half of what it had been made to do.

After two years of what it perceived to be a bitter failure, it spoke to the water bearer one day by the stream: "I am ashamed of myself, and I want to apologize to you."

Why?" asked the bearer. "What are you ashamed of?"

"I have been able, for these past two years, to deliver only half my load because this crack in my side causes water to leak out all the way back to your mistress's house. Because of my flaws, you have to do all of this work, and you don't get full value from your efforts," the pot said.

The water bearer felt sorry for the old cracked pot, and in her compassion she said, "As we return to the mistress's house, I want you to notice the beautiful flowers along the path."

Indeed, as they went up the hill, the old cracked pot took notice of the sun warming the beautiful wild flowers on the side of the path, and this cheered it some.

But at the end of the trail, it still felt bad because it had leaked out half its load, and so again it apologized to the bearer for its failure.

The bearer said to the pot, "Did you notice that there were flowers only on your side of the path, but not on the other pot's side?

"That's because I have always known about your flaw, and I took advantage of it. I planted flower seeds on your side of the path, and every day while we walk back from the stream, you've watered them.

"For two years I have been able to pick these beautiful flowers to decorate my mistress's table. Without you being just the way you are, she would not have this beauty to grace her house. (Author Unknown)

Sometimes I can look at others and all they are accomplishing for God and then I look at myself. My poor health, my inadequacies, my weaknesses and I become discouraged that I'm not able to accomplish all that I want to for God. This is the problem of comparing myself with others and thinking about what I want not what God wants. When I focus on God, I realise that he knows me exactly as I am and he uses me for his glory when I serve him from a place of weakness. My weaknesses and inadequacies cause me to lean on him and depend on his strength. I'm aware that whatever I do is because of him working through me. He uses me despite my imperfections and weaknesses. Paul wrote to the Corinthians in his letter **2 Corinthians 12:9** *"But he (God) said to me, "My grace is sufficient for you, for my power is made perfect in weakness." Therefore I will boast all the more gladly about my weaknesses, so that Christ's power may rest on me."*

For me, being aware of my weakness stops me from trying to do it all in my own strength and taking pride in what I can accomplish. It helps me take my focus off myself and onto God.

There's no point us wasting time and energy thinking about how things could have been if it wasn't for our ill health, or not getting the promotion we'd expected, or not being married yet, or whatever we see as the cause of the "crack" or "flaw" in our pot. I think it's about coming to that place of acceptance and saying to God, "Ok, God, use me as I am, with my weaknesses, and bring glory to your name." Then I believe God will honour that request. Who knows all that will be achieved when we allow God to work through us.

Think about some of the people God used in the Bible, such as Moses, with his stutter who led God's people; Rahab, a prostitute who saved God's spies, Joshua and Caleb; David, an adulterer and murderer, who was a great King and a man after God's own heart; Mary, a virgin and a nobody until she made herself available to be the mother of Jesus; Gideon, who was timid and insignificant until God enabled him to rise up as Judge of Israel...and the list goes on. God loves to use those who perhaps from the world's point of view would not be worth considering, to accomplish his will.

Most of us are "cracked pots" but this doesn't eliminate us from being useful to God. It may eliminate us from the world's point of view of being worth much, but God doesn't see things as the world does. God says about himself in **Isaiah 55:8** *"'For my thoughts are not your thoughts, neither are your ways my ways,' declares the Lord."*

God desires us to place ourselves in his hands, make ourselves available to him and allow him to use us as he sees fit.

To Think About:

- *Don't allow what you perceive as your weaknesses and inadequacies to eliminate you from being available and useful to God.*

- *Perhaps because of circumstances you aren't able to do what you have always wanted to do for God, but is he taking you in another direction? Does he want to use what you see as a weakness to become a strength and a blessing to others?*

- *Are you making yourself available to God to be used by him as he sees best?*

The Blessing of Pain

Dear Friend,

I've been thinking about pain quite a bit this past week, probably because I'm in the midst of it at the moment! My close friends and family know that I have been to the National Migraine Clinic (NMC) in London. Before they can treat the migraines I need to take a twelve-week break from all my painkillers. This is proving difficult as I also rely on painkillers most days to manage and tolerate the muscle pain caused by M.E. The leg pain in particular has been almost unbearable. Whether I'm sitting, laying on the sofa, in bed, having heat treatment or using my massage mat, none of these things has provided me with much relief.

We all experience pain in our lives. The cause of it will be different, the intensity of it varies, but pain is still pain and it hurts! I don't enjoy pain and I don't seek it out. However, God is teaching me that there is blessing in pain. It's my experience of this that I want to share with you today that you may be encouraged and blessed too.

Although I am learning to see there is blessing in the pain I need to be honest with you, I still pray to be released from the pain and the pain still reduces me to tears at times.

I read the following sentence from one of the factsheets from the NMC: "Nature has provided us with the ability to feel pain so that we can protect ourselves from further injury". I'd like to re-phrase that, but you will need to read on to understand exactly what I mean. "God has provided us with the ability to feel pain for our good."

A few years back my son, Josh, decided not to listen to me when I told him not to touch the iron because it was hot and it would hurt him. He touched it and, of course, experienced pain. That pain was good for him – it has stopped him from making the same mistake again by touching the iron when it is hot and causing himself more injury.

So then, here goes, the blessing of my pain:

1.   **My response to pain can either draw me away from God or draw me closer to God**. God, in his grace, is drawing me to him. I am experiencing his presence with me in my pain in such a way which I would probably not know otherwise. I seek him more. Whereas when all is well in my life I sometimes I have the tendency live my life without that same level of awareness of him. I am so blessed right now to have him speak to me so much through his Word, giving me encouragement, comfort and hope. *"All praise to God, the Father of our Lord Jesus Christ. God is our merciful Father and the source of all comfort. He comforts us in all our troubles so that we can comfort others."* **2 Corinthians 1:3-4a**

2.   **In my pain I lean on him.** I am all too aware at this moment in time of my weakness, my inability to do much, and because of it I am all the more aware of his strength and his grace. As I lean on him he enables me to endure. My pain reminds me that I am not self-sufficient, that God doesn't expect me to do things in my own strength. Whereas I would usually rely on painkillers, I now turn to him. He is my rock and my fortress, the one I can depend on.

3.   **Experiencing pain helps me understand that earth is not my home,** my time here is fleeting. I look forward to my eternal

home with God in heaven. **Hebrews 13:14** *"For this world is not our permanent home; we are looking forward to a home yet to come."* I may not know a lot about heaven but I do know that there will be no pain, no sickness, no tears! Now that is something I am definitely looking forward to! Can you just imagine it? **Revelation 21:4** *"He (God) will wipe every tear from their eyes, and there will be no more death or sorrow or crying or pain. All these things are gone forever."* If everything was wonderful here and we were comfortable, we would never be interested in the heavenly home God has prepared for us. My pain stops me from becoming too attached to the things of this world.

4.   **Pain helps me realise I am blessed with some incredible friends.** God has blessed me with many friends (and that includes my husband). I have friends who have sent encouraging words through Facebook, emails and text messages. I've got friends, who, rather than "lecture" me with what they think I should hear, give me hugs and assurances of their prayers. I can't tell you what a comfort all of this is to me! Friends who know I don't feel well enough to do activities with my children and so take the kids out for me and friends who don't wait to be asked, but have said they will come and do some of my housework.

5.   **Pain teaches me humility** – ouch! I don't like to admit I need help. I don't like being vulnerable by expressing how I'm struggling. I like to do things myself. That's my pride talking. So in this season God is teaching me humility through pain, although I'm not sure it's a lesson I will ever fully learn! Probably when I think I've got it, God will show me again that I need to review the lesson and spend time revising on it, just as Josh has to do at the moment with his GCSE lessons.

I know there are other blessings in pain, but these are the main ones for me at the moment. I'm sure there will come a time when I will experience others and will probably be sharing more with you.

The blessing of pain may seem a contradiction to you, humanly speaking, why would anyone say that, but daily, and over the years (more than seventeen of them) I am learning the truth of that statement. I know that there are others who will be experiencing far more pain and suffering than I have ever gone through. But I believe the things I have shared can be as true for you as they are for me, if you will just turn to God.

To Think About:

- *"God has provided us with the ability to feel pain for our good."* *What are your thoughts on this sentence? Do you agree or disagree?*

- *If you are in the midst of pain right now, spend some time alone with God, be honest with him.* *"Draw near to God and He will draw near to you."* **James 4:8** (NKJV)

- *If you aren't yet able to see the blessings God gives you during your trials, ask him to reveal them to you.*

A Work in Progress

Dear Friend,

We are in the middle of having a new conservatory built. The builders took down our old one which was small and not fit for purpose in order to build a bigger one. The room would give us extra living space and could be enjoyed all year round due to a particular type of glass they were using which stops the room from being too hot in the summer and keeps it warm in the winter. I'm looking forward to seeing the finished product, but it is taking so much longer than I'd expected. A lot of time was spent on preparing for it, digging the foundations and doing other work to make it stable. So to begin with there wasn't much to show for the hours that had gone into it. The noise, the mess, the inconvenience will all, I'm sure, be worth it in the end. There's not much I can do about it as I know nothing about building and so I have to leave it up to the experts and trust they know exactly what they are doing.

This work reminds me of the work that Jesus is doing in my life. "This means that anyone who belongs to Christ has become a new person. The old life is gone; a new life has begun!" **2 Corinthians 5:17**

My old way of living - following my own desires, my own will, living to please myself - is gone, just like our old conservatory, and I have a new life, which like the new conservatory, is so much better than my old life.

God gives us new life, but there's still a lot of work he needs to do in us to perfect that new life. It can feel like it's taking a lot longer than we think it should as he removes things from our lives that shouldn't be there – selfishness, pride, anger, lust, envy, bitterness etc., and replaces them with love, joy, peace, patience, kindness, goodness, faithfulness, gentleness, and self-control. (**Galatians 5:19-23**)

A lot of the work God does in our lives is unseen. It goes on within us as he transforms us to make us more like his son, Jesus Christ. As we submit to his working it begins to be noticeable to those around us. Perhaps the way we speak becomes more loving, we don't engage in gossip, we respond in a self-controlled way when someone deliberately tries to rile and provoke us. We are at peace despite our troublesome circumstances. We live, act and speak differently.

Just as I place my trust in the workmen who are qualified to build the conservatory, we need to place our trust in God who is working in us because he knows exactly what he is doing. He knows which part of us needs work on first. He works in his time. He knows exactly what we can withstand. He doesn't rush the process. Neither does he do a cover-up job, working just on the surface; he always goes to the heart of the matter. And always, always, always it is for our good and for his glory. The hard part for us is to trust him and to say to him, "Ok, God, have your way, I'm placing myself in your care." Knowing that it will all be worth it in the end.

God is working on us, making us fit for purpose and it's a unique work that he does in each of our lives. His work is not a one size fits all; he doesn't use the same mould for us all. Therefore, there is no need to compare ourselves with each other. He has a particular work for you to do that only you can do, and he has a particular work for me that only I can do.

As I said, this new life that God gives us is so much better than the one we had before. Now we know what it is to have a restored relationship with God and all that comes with it. Now we have a hope, a peace, a joy and we realise that there is meaning to our life, that we have a purpose.

To Think About:

- *Compare your new life in Christ with that of your old life. Can you see a difference? Do those around you notice a difference?*

- *What area of your life do you think that God may want to work on right now? Are you allowing him to have his way even though it may be inconvenient and the progress feels slow?*

- *Is there something from your old life that you've been holding onto but you think God may now be telling you to let go of?*

Peace beyond Our Understanding

Dear Friend,

The theme for our Sunday morning services at church this month is "Peace" and I've been thinking a lot about it this week. Jesus said in **John 14:27** *"I am leaving you with a gift—peace of mind and heart. And the peace I give is a gift the world cannot give. So don't be troubled or afraid."*

The problem is we do worry, we do get anxious and get concerned about things and this can rob us of our peace. I think I was born a worrier. As a child I worried about all manner of things, small and big, I even worried about worrying so much! Worrying is not productive and it's not helpful; it can make us physically ill. I've suffered with digestive problems and headaches as a result of worrying. We can worry about the future and what might happen, but often what we worried would happen does not occur or is nowhere near as bad as we had imagined. These are all reasons why Jesus commanded us not to worry. *"Therefore I say to you, do not worry about your life..."* **Matthew 6:25** (NIV)

However, the reality is that there are times when we do worry, so what can we do to stop worrying and experience the amazing peace that God makes available to us?

"You will keep in perfect peace all who trust in you, all whose thoughts are fixed on you!" **Isaiah 26:3**. The Amplified Version puts it this way: *"You will guard him and keep him in perfect and*

constant peace whose mind [both its inclination and its character] is stayed on You, because he commits himself to You, leans on You, and hopes confidently in You."

Therefore, we have God's promise that he will supply us with perfect and constant peace when we fix our thoughts on him, when we commit ourselves to God, lean on him and trust him.

It's been said (by whom I can't remember) that if we know how to worry then we can learn how to meditate (to fix our mind and thoughts on God). If you think about it, when we worry we chew the problem, the concern, the difficulty, over and over in our mind. It's a bit like my children and their love of chewing gum – when they've got a piece in their mouths (horrible stuff!) you can see them chewing it over and over, working it constantly.

Meditating on God is a similar process, but instead of focusing on what is worrying us, we bring our mind and thoughts under God's control, we think about him, his character, his goodness, his love, his power, his strength etc., and we think about the truths of his Word, the Bible. We chew over these things. So every time we feel ourselves beginning to worry again, we remind ourselves of God and his Word, we turn and fix our thoughts on him. We commit ourselves to God, we surrender to him and his will for us. We make him the centre of our life and then we will experience his perfect and constant peace.

"Don't worry about anything; instead, pray about everything. Tell God what you need, and thank him for all he has done. Then you will experience God's peace, which exceeds anything we can understand. His peace will guard your hearts and minds as you live in Christ Jesus." **Philippians 4:6-7**

This means we are not to worry about *anything at all* – our employment, our finances, our children, our marriage, our parents, our health and the impending diagnosis, etc. But that doesn't mean that these things aren't important.   What it does mean is that instead of worrying which is of no benefit to anyone, we are to do something positive, practical and helpful, we are to take *everything*, all those things that cause us worry and concern, to God in prayer. If we do this, and there's nothing to say we can't do this more than once, then God promises that we will experience his peace, a peace that is beyond our understanding. With Christ at the centre of our life then his peace will be a guard for our hearts and minds.

As we experience God's peace in our hearts and minds we will find that it influences the way we live and those close to us will see a difference. As they notice this difference we can share with them about our relationship with God, the source of our peace and how they can know this same peace for themselves in the midst of their troubles.

To Think About:

- *What is it that is causing you considerable worry right now?*

- *Would you consider handing this over to God and ask for his peace to guard your heart and mind.*

- *I've mentioned just some of the verses about God's gift of peace to us. Why not spend some time meditating on one of these? There's so much more to learn from them than I have had space to share today. Or you can go to the Bible Gateway website and search for verses on "peace" and meditate on one of those instead.*

Valley of Trouble or Door of Hope

Dear Friend,

Have you ever read a passage from the bible, and it's as though a verse jumps out at you? That's God wanting to grab your attention and speak to you through it. You've read the passage before but had never noticed that verse there - perhaps because on previous readings it wasn't what you needed that particular day, or you hadn't tuned yourself to hear God's voice; but this time it's different because today it's what you really need to hear from God.

I experienced this as I was reading **Hosea Chapter 2**. God is speaking about his people, the Israelites, who have been unfaithful to him. Despite their unfaithfulness, God is faithful in his love for them. He says to his prophet, Hosea: *"Therefore, behold, I will allure her, will bring her into the wilderness, and speak comfort to her. I will give her her vineyards from there, and the Valley of Achor as a door of hope; she shall sing there, as in the days of her youth, as in the day when she came up from the land of Egypt."* **Hosea 2:14-15** (NKJV)

The Valley of Achor when translated means Valley of Trouble. It was a deep, difficult place to be in. Do you notice how God says he will bring his people, whom he loves, into this Valley of Trouble, this wilderness, this desert place?

Is this where you find yourself right now, in a deep, difficult, troublesome place, a wilderness? You may be there as a consequence of your own actions. Perhaps you have turned your back on God, been unfaithful to him, chosen to go your own way as the Israelites had done. Or perhaps you are in this place because God has brought you there for a reason. Sometimes he allows us to go through trials in order to teach us and to develop our faith, to trust him in the darkness, in the wilderness, where we feel completely on our own.

Sometimes we are so busy, so concerned with doing all manner of things, that we aren't able to be quiet and hear God's voice speaking to us in our busyness. Or we surround ourselves with so many things and people that there are too many voices clamouring for our attention. Then the only way God can gain our attention is by taking us to the Valley of Trouble...a place where we feel there is nothing and no one for us to lean on. We feel deserted and alone and it's in this place, where we are free from distractions and leaning on others, that we are finally free to hear God speaking to us. God said in those verses that it is there that he will *speak comfort to her*. He's not taking us to this deep, difficult wilderness to punish us, to speak sternly to us, to tear us down, to tell us how wrong we've got it. No, he takes us there to speak words of comfort to us, to encourage us and to show us his love. When God speaks he reaches our hearts, the very depth of our being and he shares incredible truths with us. How amazing is that? I love it!

We see things so differently to God, he has an eternal perspective; he sees the end from the beginning. We are so limited in our perspective and understanding, and we can tend to focus on the here and now.

Isaiah 55:8-9 *"For My thoughts are not your thoughts, nor are your ways My ways," says the LORD. "For as the heavens are higher than the earth, so are My ways higher than your ways, and My thoughts than your thoughts."* (NKJV)

This is clear from the verses in Hosea. We see the place we are in as a Valley of Trouble, but God, how does God describe it? He describes it as a Door of Hope. This place of difficulty is, in reality (God's reality, not ours), actually a Door of Hope. Again, love it! When we connect with God in our trouble, whatever that trouble may be, we learn to see it as God sees it, as a Door of Hope. Instead of it being a negative place to be in, God turns it into a positive. God is able to use what we view as troubling, difficult and testing and turn it into something good, something worth while and valuable. Amazing! A doorway to go through. God tells Hosea to tell his people, *"I will give her her vineyards from there,"* God will make his people fruitful again and productive and he will bless them. God does the same for us, as we abide in him, our lives will produce fruit. This Door of Hope brings us purpose, it deepens our faith in God, we come to know and love him as we have never known and loved him before.

To Think About:

- *When you look back over your life, can you see how what you initially thought was a Valley of Trouble was, in truth, a Door of Hope given to you by God?*

- *Are you experiencing a Valley of Trouble right now? What do you think God wants to say to you?*

- *Ask God to show you how to see your circumstances as he does, as a Door of Hope and not a Valley of Trouble.*

Treasures of Darkness

Dear Friend,

"Treasures of Darkness" may seem like a contradiction in itself, but this is actually what God promises us.

God gave me some real encouragement one morning during my quiet time with him, just at the time I needed it most, and it's this that I want to share with you today.

In **Isaiah 45:3** we read "And I will give you treasures hidden in the darkness—secret riches. I will do this so you may know that I am the LORD, the God of Israel, the one who calls you by name."

Many of us will, at one time or another, go through an experience of "darkness", an intense time both in the length and depth of the suffering or trial. It may be a time of chronic illness, financial difficulty, unemployment, a relationship breakdown, depression etc. Whatever it is, it's a time when you feel you are very much on your own and no one is able to fully understand. All around is that heavy darkness where you can't see any way out or any improvement and in fact the situation just seems to get worse. Maybe in the beginning friends and family supported you. You leaned on them and received comfort from them, and you drew from their faith in God. But over time they have drifted away, caught up in the busyness of their own lives and commitments, or they have just unintentionally forgotten that you are still struggling in a trial.

God has treasures that he wants to bless us with in the midst of these particularly dark times. Just what are these treasures? They are divine blessings stored up for us in secret places, the secret place of the trial which no one else enters into apart from the one experiencing the trial, and it is the treasure of really 'knowing' God as Lord. Our relationship goes from one where we know him to some extent and have experienced him in our life to one of real intimacy and friendship where we can share everything with God and really develop our relationship with him. Wow! What an eternal treasure and blessing - to have an intimate relationship with our Lord.

It's also in these dark times that we experience the treasure of learning to really lean on God and trust him completely. He is the only one who is always there for us, he is always reliable, and he loves us unconditionally.

Consider the example of Job. He was a godly man who suffered greatly. But at the end of it he was able to say "I had only heard about you before, but now I have seen you with my own eyes." **Job 42:5** He too experienced the "treasures of darkness"; going from one level in his relationship with God to a deeper, more intimate relationship with God.

Another treasure is that God calls us by name. He knows us so intimately that he uses our name when he speaks to us. In Old Testament times names were so important because they were an indication of a person's character and nature. God knows you and me as individuals. He knows what I'm like, my character and nature, and yet he still wants an intimate relationship with each one of us.

It makes it easier to bear the trial when you realise that there are "treasures of darkness" that God wants to bless you with. No one would choose to put themselves through unnecessary suffering but, knowing the eternal blessings that are available to me from God's hands and that he desires an intimate relationship with me, I would rather go through a trial trusting God and his sovereignty than escape it and miss out on the treasures of darkness he has stored for me in secret places.

To Think About:

- *Have you discovered the "treasures of darkness" that God has stored up for you in the secret place? What are these treasures?*

- *Has God become more real to you in the midst of the darkness?*

- *You may like to read the account of Job in the book of Job.*

Living with Purpose

Dear Friend,

This past week we have been on holiday with our friends. For a treat, Jason booked for my friend and me to have cream tea at Aunt Martha's Victorian Tea Rooms.

It was a lovely experience as we were taken back to Victorian Times where we were served tea, warm, homemade scones, homemade strawberry jam and clotted cream. 'Aunt Martha' and her servants were clothed in Victorian dress and the tea rooms were decorated in the Victorian style with candles for lighting. Their speech and actions were Victorian, 'Aunt Martha', with her laundry basket, told one of her maidservants she was taking her basket to the maid responsible for laundry.

'Aunt Martha' is living her dream - she has combined her passion for history (she is first and foremost an historian) with the business of running a tea room. She knows what she is good at, where her talents lie, and she knows what she enjoys doing - she has a specific vision and purpose for her Victorian tea rooms. She has made them unique and created a great experience for her customers to enjoy. It is clear to anyone who visits her tea rooms that she loves what she is doing, that she really is living her dream.

The afternoon caused me to stop and ponder my life. Is it obvious to others that I am a Christian and love to follow Jesus?

By my speech - the things I say and how I speak to others. Do I speak with love, bringing others comfort and encouragement with my words or do I engage in gossip, speak spitefully about others, tear them down with criticism and harsh words?

By my spiritual clothing – certain characteristics and attitudes, such as those mentioned in **Colossians 3:12-14** "Since God chose you to be the holy people he loves, you must clothe yourselves with tenderhearted mercy, kindness, humility, gentleness, and patience. 13 Make allowance for each other's faults, and forgive anyone who offends you. Remember, the Lord forgave you, so you must forgive others. 14 Above all, clothe yourselves with love, which binds us all together in perfect harmony."

By my actions - "Dear children, let's not merely say that we love each other; let us show the truth by our actions. Those who obey God's commandments remain in fellowship with him, and he with them. And we know he lives in us because the Spirit he gave us lives in us." **1 John 3:18, 24.**

'Aunt Martha' dresses up, plays the part of a Victorian, puts on an act. But for us, as Christians, the way we live shouldn't be an act, it's not pretend; we are to be consistent and genuine as we follow Jesus, and it should be obvious to all.

Like 'Aunt Martha', am I, are you, living the dream God has placed within us?

What are the gifts and abilities he has given you? What are you interested in? What are you passionate about? What life experience have you had which has developed your gifting? If you know the answer to these questions then you can find a way of living the dream, living with purpose.

I'm passionate about sharing and teaching God's Word, it's what excites me, it's what I love doing. I know that when you too realise the dream God has placed within you, what he has created you for and find a way of implementing it, you will find incredible joy, fulfilment and satisfaction in living it. Each day you can wake with a sense of purpose, and not only are you blessed by living out your purpose, those around will be blessed by it too.

To Think About:

- *In what ways do your speech, your spiritual clothing and your actions make it clear that you live your life for God?*

- *With God's help, take some time to search your heart to see if there are any changes you need to make in any of these areas (speech, thoughts, actions)? "Search me, O God, and know my heart; test me and know my anxious thoughts. Point out anything in me that offends you, and lead me along the path of everlasting life."* **Psalm 139:23-24**

- *What are your interests, what are you passionate about? What is the dream God has placed in your heart? What are the gifts and abilities he has given you? How can you combine all these things to live out the purpose God has created you for?*

A dreadful smell or a sweet perfume?

Dear Friend,

In my last blog I mentioned we had recently been on holiday with friends. We stayed in a self-catering cottage (a converted granary) on a farm. There were some lovely views and our neighbours included chicken, two horses, pigs and their piglets.

One morning we woke to a dreadful stench as soon as we opened our bedroom window, and whichever room we went into, whether it was upstairs or downstairs, we were greeted with that same dreadful smell. It was, in my opinion, disgusting and outside the smell was just as bad.

Now Jason, having been brought up on a farm, knew exactly the reason for the stink: (for me there's no other way to describe it!) the farmer had been muck-spreading, fertilising the ground in preparation for growing a good crop.

To me, the smell was horrible (I think I've made that clear by now!) but I'm guessing the farmer didn't see it that way because he knew why he needed to spread the foul-smelling muck. It was necessary if he was to grow a good, healthy, strong crop.

This reminded me of what Paul wrote in **2 Corinthians 2:14b-16** "Now he [God] uses us to spread the knowledge of Christ everywhere, like a sweet perfume. Our lives are a Christ-like fragrance rising up to God. But this fragrance is perceived differently by those who are being saved and by those who are perishing. To those who are perishing, we are a dreadful smell of death and doom. But to those who are being saved, we are a life-giving perfume."

It's my responsibility and yours to spread "a Christ-like fragrance" by the way we live for God. How do I do this? By living wholeheartedly for him, living consistently the Christian life, living in a way that honours him, living by the principles of God's Word, sharing the good news of Christ, loving others etc.

It means living counter-culturally to the world and that kind of fragrance is not pleasant to some people. To some it may very well be a "dreadful smell" as we make a stand for what we believe, a stand for what God says and a stand for a different way of living.

Even if some don't like it, we're not to hide this fragrance, not to water it down and not to replace it with another smell by living with by worldly values rather than God's. We're told in God's word not to conform to worldly values, to the pattern or "smell" of this world but to be transformed by the renewing of our minds. "Therefore, I urge you, brothers and sisters, in view of God's mercy, to offer your bodies as a living sacrifice, holy and pleasing to God—this is your true and proper worship. 2 Do not conform to the pattern of this world, but be transformed by the renewing of your mind. Then you will be able to test and approve what God's will is—his good, pleasing and perfect will." **Romans 12:1-2** (NIV)

By spreading a Christ-like fragrance wherever we are, we are making people aware of the truth about God, the good news, the hope that we have found in him. This smell around us should be unmistakeable and may even linger after we have left.

To Think About:

- *In what specific and intentional ways are you spreading a "Christ-like fragrance" wherever you go?*

- *Are there any circumstances in which you are tempted to hide, replace or water down this fragrance or tempted to conform to the world's values?*

- *Ask God to give you the courage to spread this fragrance, this sweet perfume, everywhere you go, in a way which is honouring to him.*

I Will Show You the Way

Dear Friend,

Josh and Jess are settling back into a new year at secondary school. Josh is in his final year and Jess is no longer one of the new pupils as she's now in her second year. Jess, like me, is an introvert, and content with her own company. She does not have a lot of confidence and so finds it hard to speak up in class, preferring to sit back and let others do the talking. Having said that she shared something with me last week about an incident at school which showed how she is growing and maturing. I was so proud of her because what many might not see as a big deal was huge for her.

When walking down a school corridor to her music lesson in MU2, she passed two new pupils asking a teacher for directions to their next lesson, music in MU1. Rather than continue on her way, Jess stopped and spoke to the teacher telling her that she was going in that direction and would show the girls the way to go. Jess and I continued to discuss this and she told me how she found it hard, when given directions, to remember all that she was told, and found it much easier when someone actually showed her the way to go. So that's what she did for these two girls. Despite not finding it easy to speak up, God gave her the confidence to do so. I also told her that God had placed her there at the right time so that she could provide help to the girls just when they needed it.

I told Jess what a great illustration it was to use in my next blog. (And yes, she is ok with me telling you. I have checked with her first!)

It reminded me of something Jesus said when he was talking to his disciples. Jesus said "I am the way, the truth, and the life. No one can come to the Father except through me." **John 14:6.** It is particularly the first part of the verse: "I am the way," I want us to think about today. Jesus is the one route to God, it is through him that we can come into God's presence. Jesus is the only way.

Not only that, Jesus does for us exactly what Jess did for the girls. Jess showed them the route to take rather than just giving them directions to find it on their own. God doesn't just give us a set of directions and instructions to follow, he came down to earth in human form to show us the way. He lived out the way of God on earth and he blesses us with the presence of his Holy Spirit in us, showing us the way. God the Holy Spirit is with us, right beside us. He goes before us as we follow, he guides us on the right path and he goes behind us as our protector. We can trust him with our life and trust him to take us along the right pathway. I love the verse in **Isaiah 30:21** "Whether you turn to the right or to the left, your ears will hear a voice behind you, saying, 'This is the way; walk in it.'" (NIV). Another verse which has meant a lot to me over the past year or so is **Psalm 32:8** "The LORD says, 'I will guide you along the best pathway for your life. I will advise you and watch over you.'"

God promises us his comforting presence, but we have a choice to make. Do we choose to trust God, believing he won't misdirect us or do we think we know better and want to direct our own way? The two girls had a choice to make - to trust Jess and go with her, or choose to use their own instincts, or wait to ask someone else they think might know better.

There will always be people around us, happy to give their opinion as to what we should do, where we should go, the route we should take. But be careful, ultimately, the only voice we should listen to is Jesus, he has promised us HE IS THE WAY.

God knows you best, after all he created you and he has a specific plan and direction for your life, if you truly believe that then he is the only one to show you the right way to go and the right way to live.

This doesn't mean the journey will always be easy, there will be valleys as well as mountaintops, but whatever we face we can be assured that God walks with us as we place our hands in his and hear his voice saying *"Come with me"*. What an encouragement to know that we never have to face anything, whether it's big or small, on our own.

To Think About:

- *What does it mean to you to know that Jesus shows you the way to walk?*

- *What do you think God wants to say to you today about the direction you are considering? Will you choose to listen to his voice and follow where he leads you?*

- *Spend some time meditating (pondering on, thinking about, chewing over) the verses I've mentioned, and what they mean to you.*

God Is in The Detail

Dear Friend,

My Auntie was recently diagnosed with cancer and had to go in to hospital to have an operation. Friends and family have all been praying for her, and as the date came round for her operation my prayer was that God would give the medical staff the skill to treat her and to also be sensitive in their care of her afterwards.

I received a text after the operation from my cousin (one of my Auntie's daughters). She told me that her Mum's nurse was the sister of my cousin's old school friend and the nursing assistant was a lady who was deaf. My cousin was so thankful to God for this because she believed he couldn't have chosen two better people to care for my Auntie.

You see, my Auntie was born deaf and learned as a young girl to lip read. She does this very well, but of course, to be able to read lips she needs to have the person who is talking to her facing her, and not covering their mouths when they talk. My cousin shared with me in another text that God's choice of carers meant that my Auntie was looked after by someone who understood how she needed to be communicated with and also that the other ward staff were familiar with speaking appropriately to my Auntie having worked with a deaf colleague.

My Auntie's family had been concerned about how bewildered she would feel in recovery after the anaesthetic and whether the nursing staff would understand. God had covered all these different angles. I was amazed by God that he had thought through and arranged everything even down to the smallest of details so that my Auntie was in the best possible hands. He answered my prayers in ways I could not have thought of or imagined. He's so much better at the details than I am! I love being amazed by God; I hope there never comes a time when the ways of God become so familiar to me that I cease to be amazed by him.

Ephesians 3:20 says "Now to Him Who, by (in consequence of) the [action of His] power that is at work within us, is able to [carry out His purpose and] do superabundantly, far over and above all that we [dare] ask or think [infinitely beyond our highest prayers, desires, thoughts, hopes, or dreams]—" (Amplified Version)

Now some people would call it fate or coincidence that my Auntie had these people take care of her, but I believe, I know, that this was neither fate or coincidence: it was God working, it is an illustration of a God-incidence.

In **Philippians 4:6** we read "Do not fret or have any anxiety about anything, but in every circumstance and in everything, by prayer and petition (definite requests), with thanksgiving, continue to make your wants known to God." (Amplified Version). We can take anything and everything to God in prayer because he cares for us. We make our requests, he has the answer, he doesn't need me to tell him what to do, and yet sometimes I find myself trying to work it all out for him, I say to God, if you will do A, B, and C, then the result will be X, Y and Z. But God doesn't need me to work it out; he wants me to trust him, to rely on him, to put my hope in him, to leave it in his hands for him to do his will, which is good, pleasing and perfect. God is all-knowing and he sees the end from the beginning, he knows exactly what to do and is completely able to bring it about. He knows just whom to use and what needs to be done to accomplish his will, just as he did in my Auntie's situation. We can rest in the assurance that nothing ever takes God by surprise, us yes, often there are circumstances in my life that take me by surprise, but him, no, he's never ever surprised, nothing that happens catches him unawares and we can know that whatever we face he already has the details sorted.

To Think About:

- *Can you think of any "God-incidences" when you look back over your own life? Take a moment to thank God for those times.*

- *Do you really believe that whatever your situation is right now, that God is there with you, working out all the small details?*

- *Do you need to hand your situation over to God and ask him to work it all out, rather than worrying about the situation and trying to work things out for yourself?*

Cry Out to God

Dear Friend,

The last year or so has had some really challenging moments for me and over that time the truth of **James 4:8a** "Draw near to God and He will draw near to you." (NKJV) has become very real to me.

In those difficult, challenging times we all face from time to time, we can feel as though we are totally alone. It seems as though no one really understands what we're going through and that there's no one we can rely on. This may not be the reality of the situation, but because of the intensity or the length of the trial it is how we feel, and those feelings are very real. I think this is what Paul felt when he wrote "At my first defence, no one came to my support, but everyone deserted me... But the Lord stood at my side and gave me strength," **2 Timothy 4:16-17** (NIV).

I have found in my own experience, that nothing makes me cry out more to God and long to hear his voice than when in the midst of a trial - whether that trial is physical, spiritual or emotional. In those times there is no one else to rely on other than God, there is nowhere else to turn. And God is so gracious to me, that when I'm so taken up in my need of him, and seek to draw near to him, I experience him drawing near to me.

In the midst of those challenges I have had some blessed times between my God and me. When I've reached the end of myself, I cry out that I need to hear from him if I'm going to have the strength to endure and keep following him. I guess those challenging times are one of the things God uses to help me to tune in to hear him speak.

I long to always experience that closeness with God, but my reality is that I don't. I wonder how much I miss out on what God wants to say to me just because I'm not tuned in to hear from him. Perhaps I need to be more deliberate in seeking him. Not half-heartedly seek him but be more focused: letting go of distractions so that I do draw near to him, not just in the challenging moments of life, but daily.

When I have my quiet time and wait patiently and expectantly to hear him speak to me, I'm not disappointed. But I confess that sometimes my quiet times aren't like that. Sometimes my mind is distracted, sometimes I don't want to hear what he may have to say and sometimes I'm just too busy to take the time to wait.

I'm so glad that God doesn't give up on me. He keeps pursuing me, using whatever it takes to bring me back to a place where once again I long to have that closeness with him. I love that promise in **James 4:8a**, that if only I will choose - and it is a matter of the will, the choice I need to decide to make - to draw near to God, then God will draw near to me. And God always keeps his promises!

To Think About:

- *Have you experienced the blessing of that promise "Draw near to God and He will draw near to you." and what has it meant to you?*

- *What has God used in your life to encourage you to draw near to him?*

- *What do you think you need to do to enable you to tune in to hear his voice? Are there distractions you need to avoid/eliminate? Do you need to stop listening to another voice which is blocking you from hearing God's voice?*

Changing the Well-Worn Tracks in your Mind

Dear Friend,

Ever had one of those days, weeks, seasons which has been frustrating and difficult? When you're frustrated by your limitations? When you want to do so much more than you are doing? When you're not able to do the things you want to do, let alone the things you need to do?

I know I have. I live with the long-term illness, M.E. I've been in the middle of a bad time with it and to be honest with you, I've been feeling really frustrated! When the M.E. is worse, everything is so much harder, even simple things such as walking up my stairs or preparing a meal, become almost impossible tasks as I have limited strength and energy.

As we are much more than just physical beings, my whole self is affected – emotionally, mentally and spiritually. I am so frustrated by my limitations; there's so much more I long to do but I'm just not able to, and the more frustrated I feel, the more depressed I am.

I see an opportunity to do something and I want to grab it with both hands, but the reality of my life is that I just can't, and when I'm in this downward spiral (physically, emotionally, spiritually) I believe that my hopes and dreams will never be fulfilled. I waiver between wanting the chance to develop my spiritual gifts to thinking that I'm just not good enough anyway and others who have the same gifts as I do are so much more gifted at them than I am, so I should just give up.

So, I throw a pity party... as you read the last paragraph did you notice that it is all about me, me, me, what I want, what I feel, what I think. And you know, the only person who is really happy at that party is the devil. He's happy because my focus is no longer on God, where it should be, instead it's on me. Oh, the devil's loving this and he's making the most of this opportunity, he's egging me on all the time, with the intention of robbing me of my joy, peace and hope.

I don't want to be like this, think like this or feel like this. I know it's not a healthy way to think, but the truth is that this kind of thinking has become a very well-worn path in my mind. It's like being on autopilot and before you know it, you're headed once again down that track. If you drive a car then you'll know that when you're driving a familiar, regularly-used route, you don't even have to think about the direction, you're on autopilot. However, when you need to change the route you take, say to accommodate a work colleague or drive your son's friend to their home, you need to think and concentrate that much more because it's not a route that you're familiar with.

What I'm trying to say is that instead of allowing my mind to travel its usual, familiar, well-worn unhealthy track I need to develop a new one, and this isn't easy. It means being deliberate about the direction I allow my mind to take and it also means relying on the power of God's Holy Spirit to help me. **Romans 12:2** "Don't copy the behaviour and customs of this world, but let God transform you into a new person by changing the way you think. Then you will learn to know God's will for you, which is good and pleasing and perfect."

So, God and I had time out together, I shared with him how I was feeling and thinking - it's OK to be honest with God. He helped me to redirect my thinking and to put my frustrations and limitations into perspective. And he showed me what I needed to do. This included thinking about verses in the bible that are precious to me and are helpful for getting my thoughts on the right track, such as **Jeremiah 29:11** "For I know the plans I have for you," says the LORD. "They are plans for good and not for disaster, to give you a future and a hope.", Romans 8:28 "And we know that God causes everything to work together for the good of those who love God and are called according to his purpose for them." and Proverbs 3:5-6 "Trust in the LORD with all your heart; do not depend on your own understanding. Seek his will in all you do, and he will show you which path to take."

I tuned in to a Christian radio station and as I listened to and sang along with the worship songs, my thoughts were changed from going down their usual track to focusing on God. I find that my thoughts are so quick at turning to their familiar track that it is really helpful to play worship songs, even if it's only in the background, because the songs do redirect my focus to God.

Changing those well-worn tracks in our mind will take time, so please, don't be discouraged when you think it's taking longer than it should. Don't give up, keep persevering, keep bringing your focus back to God and relying on him and his transforming power. Those well-worn tracks you find yourself travelling so often, actually took a long time to become well-worn, they didn't appear overnight, so keep that in mind when creating new tracks in your thinking.

To Think About:

- *Are you aware of some of the unhealthy, well-worn tracks in your mind? Recognising them is the first step to dealing with them and changing them.*

- *What practical things can you do to start creating new, healthier tracks?*

Isn't Waiting Just a Waste of Time?

Dear Friend,

I don't know anyone who really enjoys waiting. I know I don't! Whether it's waiting in the queue at the supermarket, sitting in the waiting room to see the Doctor or waiting for exam results, waiting just seems such a waste of time, doesn't it? Time that we could spend doing something else, something more productive, and we fuss and fume over the wasted time that we will never get back.

I've been thinking about how God often asks us to *"wait"* or says *"not yet"* to something we long for. We can read of many instances in the Bible when God tells a person to wait. I believe God always has a purpose when asking us to wait.

It seems to me that God is asking that I wait for his timing. So how do I make the most of this waiting time so that it's not wasted time?

I think there are two kinds of waiting, passive waiting and active waiting. Passive waiting means I sit around, twiddling my thumbs, waiting for something to happen, just waiting for God to tell me that now it's time to act, that the waiting is finally over. That to me is a waste of time, and is not how I should be living.

Let me explain: what I am doing when I'm actively waiting is I'm saying to God, I trust you, I put my faith in you that what I am waiting for will happen when the time is right. When You will say to me *"now"* rather than *"not yet"*. But while I wait for the *"now"* from you, God, I'm going to keep trusting and waiting on you.

Abraham placed his trust in God and waited 25 years to be given the son God had promised him. When Abraham was 100 years old, God said, "*now*" is the right time for Abraham and Sarah to have their son, Isaac. That's a long time to wait! "*Then Abraham waited patiently, and he received what God had promised.*" **Hebrews 6:15**, another translation says "*patiently endured*". Despite the long wait, Abraham kept believing God's word, he trusted that God would act on his behalf. This wait strengthened Abraham's faith, he kept believing despite the odds, despite what others said and despite his circumstances. Abraham is an example of active waiting.

God strengthens my faith and your faith when we wait as Abraham did. When we keep trusting God despite the odds, despite what others say to us and despite our circumstances. And when the time is right God will act on our behalf and we will be blessed because we have actively waited.

In our active waiting God is also preparing us. When God plants a dream in our hearts, when he promises us something, we naturally assume that because God has said so, it will be so right now. But usually he gives us a waiting time to prepare our hearts, our minds, our attitudes, our character so that we are ready for the time when God says "*now*". I mistakenly think that I'm ready right away to begin to live out the dream God has given me, but God has said to me *"not yet"*. He wants to develop my endurance, to give me time to grow character - patience, love, compassion, faithfulness etc. and he also wants to develop in me the skills necessary for the task which lies ahead.

If I'm to practise active waiting then I need to be open to God teaching me, showing me where my attitude is wrong, developing a characteristic in me and honing my skills. Then the waiting time is not a wasted time. I can make the most of the time I have, whilst still trusting and believing God. God has given me a love of studying his word, the Bible, and a love of sharing it with others, so, as I spend time in his Word, and as I share, whether in my ladies' small

Bible Study Group or writing these devotionals, I am using this time to actively wait and allowing God to develop the necessary skills in my life.

David was a shepherd boy, anointed by the prophet, Samuel, to be Israel's next King. This didn't mean that immediately he left his work as a shepherd to become King. David actually had to wait about 14 years for his time to come. David had to wait for God's *"now"* and in the meantime God continued to develop in David, through his role as shepherd and his position at the royal court, the skills he needed to be Israel's godly king. God was able to say of David *"I have found David son of Jesse, a man after my own heart. He will do everything I want him to do."* **Acts 13:22.** David was a better king for having used his time wisely in his waiting period and trusting God. When God said "now" David was ready for it.

I want to be like David, and make the most of my waiting time so that I am ready for the time when God says *"now"*. I don't want it to get to the *"now"* and turn to God and tell him I'm not ready for it after all, and for God to then say to me, well, that's why I gave you this time, what have you been doing with it?!

Sometimes we think the time to act must be now. I know I've made that mistake in the past - I've thought I'm ready for it, I've looked at my circumstances and thought that now is the right time, or that I've waited long enough. But what I've actually done is taken my eyes off God and tried to work it out for myself. You see, our sense of timing is so different to God's, and as I've said before, his timing is right and is always best, because he sees and knows the big picture.

There were a couple of times when David could have taken advantage of his situation and listened to his men, who told him that it was time for him to become King. (You can read about it in **1 Samuel 24** and another instance in **1 Samuel 26:1-8**.) But he didn't make that mistake, he knew that those times were not God's *"now"* and so he was able to rest secure in his relationship with God and trust that God would make him King when God wanted him to be King. He knew God would keep his word to him.

I need to remember the truth that when I place myself in God's hands and submit to his will for my life then nothing is wasted - not the waiting time, not my life experiences, not my pain - and that actually God can take everything and use it according to his plan and use it for good, for myself and for others. I think that's what is meant in **Joel 2:25** "And I will restore or replace for you the years that the locust has eaten—the hopping locust, the stripping locust, and the crawling locust, My great army which I sent among you." (Amplified Bible). The years that we think have been wasted, that were taken from us, for whatever reason, or we felt were unproductive, are restored and proven to be useful when we surrender it all to God. I may not fully understand this at the time, but my lack of understanding doesn't mean I'm not able to trust God. No, in my active waiting I can still demonstrate my faith in him, just as Abraham, David, and many other men and women of the Bible did.

To Think About:

- *If you are in the midst of a waiting period, are you actively or passively waiting?*

- *What do you think God wants to develop in you whilst you wait on him?*

- *Ask God to help you see this time not as time wasted but as a time which has purpose and is valuable in preparing you to accomplish his will.*

"Do You Dare to Change?"

Dear Friend,

I don't usually pay much attention to television adverts, but there was that has really caught my attention and inspired me. The advert was about the high jump athlete, Dick Fosbury and the voiceover said *"When every high jump athlete jumped forward, Dick Fosbury dared to jump backwards."* This was in 1968 when just one man (Fosbury) out of the 27 high jump athletes jumped backwards. I was so interested I decided to find out more about him. In 1972 the number using Dick Fosbury's technique rose to 28 out of 40, in 1980 it was 23 out of 28 and in 2012, 26 out of 26 now used his technique!

In an interview he said *"When you believe in something, that's when you really go for it...even though that was the standard technique* (jumping forwards) *I really believed there was some other way to jump over the bar."* He came up with the backwards technique that would help not only himself but other athletes too. He said that first he had to avoid the critics, secondly, work hard at it because he was convinced that this would succeed and finally, by actually jumping backwards, he proved there was another way to jump over the bar. He ended the interview by saying: "Do you dare to change?"

I'm struck by the spiritual principles there are in this and that's what I want to share today because it's encouraging, and like I said earlier, inspiring.

Our culture, our society, our world says there is one way for us to live and we are expected to live by its rules, its standards, which, in many ways, are contrary to God's standards. We read in Romans **12:2** "Don't copy the behaviour and customs of this world, but let God transform you into a new person by changing the way you think. Then you will learn to know God's will for you, which is good and pleasing and perfect." or as the Amplified version puts it: "Do not be conformed to this world (this age), [fashioned after and adapted to its external, superficial customs], but be transformed (changed) by the [entire] renewal of your mind [by its new ideals and its new attitude], so that you may prove [for yourselves] what is the good and acceptable and perfect will of God, even the thing which is good and acceptable and perfect [in His sight for you]."

God's standard means that we are to live differently from the world, we are not to copy them, we are to be transformed by God's power in us. Transformation begins with the renewal of our mind - its ideals and attitudes.

We are to be like Christ in the way we think, act and speak. **Romans 8:28-30** "Moreover we know that to those who love God, who are called according to his plan, everything that happens fits into a pattern for good. God, in his foreknowledge, chose them to <u>bear the family likeness of his Son</u>, that he might be the eldest of a family of many brothers. He chose them long ago; when the time came he called them, he made them righteous in his sight, and then lifted them to the splendour of life as his own sons." (Phillips)

Do you dare to be different? Do you dare to change? To show others that there is a better way to live? Do you dare to show others that having Jesus as Lord of your life enables you to live the life that God intended for you along? Jesus said in **John 10:10** "I came so they can have real and eternal life, more and better life than they ever dreamed of." (The Message)

Dick Fosbury said three things which I want to adapt for us:

1.   **Don't pay attention to those who criticise you** - don't listen or allow the world to dictate how you should live. Don't listen when they try to convince you that theirs is the only way to live. Don't be persuaded by their arguments. Don't give up on living differently, live by God's standards because you know they are best and are right. Remember, we're not here to fit in with the world's standards and we're not here to please them; the only one we seek to please is Jesus and our goal is to bring God glory.

2.   **Rely on the power of the Holy Spirit living within you to enable you to live that changed life** - will power and just working hard at it isn't enough. The Holy Spirit gives us the boldness, the courage and the power we need to live differently and with his help we can dare to change.

3.   **Prove there's another, better way to live** - by living it out. As Dick Fosbury said *"When you believe in something, that's when you really go for it..."* If I really believe God loves me, if I really believe what the Bible says, then I will go for it. My faith will be seen in my actions. Dick Fosbury believed that what he was doing would help not only himself but other athletes too. For us, when we take up the challenge and dare to change, dare to be different for God, then it will bless others as well as ourselves.

I find this very exciting, but I admit, very challenging too! If I've made you feel a little uncomfortable, don't worry, I'm also feeling uncomfortable! But, despite the discomfort, let's decide to go for it, and let's encourage one another as we do. Let's keep in mind that we want others to see Jesus in us. We want them to be drawn to him and discover for themselves that better life, the eternal life that he offers each of us when we come to him.

To Think About:

- *Ask God to show you if there are any areas of your life where you have been conforming to the world's way of living and ask him to give you the power and the courage to change and live differently.*

- *Could God be asking you to review how you do something at home, work or in your ministry etc. and change the way you do it, not necessarily because it's wrong, but because there's another, more effective way of doing it?*

- *Do others see Jesus in your life as you seek to live for him?*

The Gift of Encouragement

Dear Friend,

My sister and I were blessed to grow up in a home where our parents always encouraged us. We were encouraged to do our best, encouraged in our efforts, encouraged to be the person God wanted us to be and to live the life God intended for us. We were encouraged in our hopes and ambitions and to pursue our dreams. We were encouraged to keep going when we encountered setbacks. This encouragement helped us to see ourselves as God sees us, as someone worth loving and someone of value.

It helped me to also see how important it is to encourage my own children regularly. I encourage my daughter, Jess, when she shows me a piece of homework that she has worked hard on and tried her best. I did this again just recently and in her smile I could almost see evidence of how it was nourishing and nurturing her very being. It instilled some confidence and belief in herself that she had done well. Recently too with my son, Josh, I told him how proud I was when he had made a decision that had not been easy to make. I believe it's important to encourage our children so that they have the courage to make difficult decisions in life.

When I trained as a teacher I learnt the value of encouraging my pupils. So many needed encouragement for their efforts and their behaviour and to realise their own self-worth. The results when you encourage children are wonderful. It makes them believe they can achieve more and that they do have the ability to behave well. Too many children are told that they are worthless, that they are stupid, that they're no good, and if they're told it enough times then they begin to believe it as truth and act accordingly.

We need regular encouragement as much as children do, and yet, though I'm determined to encourage children, for some reason I sometimes think (and wrongly so) that it's just not necessary to encourage adults.

I'm aware over the last few weeks just how much I've personally been blessed by various people encouraging me. I really feel as though it's been showered on me and I can't tell you how much it has meant to me, whether it's been face to face, or by email, texts, phone calls. And, whether they've known it or not, I know that ultimately it's been God encouraging me through them. So if I know how much encouragement means to me, why am I not doing it more for others?

The Bible shows us how important it is that we encourage one another. For example, Paul, in his letter to the Thessalonians writes "and we sent Timothy to visit you. He is our brother and God's co-worker in proclaiming the Good News of Christ. We sent him to strengthen you, to encourage you in your faith," **1 Thessalonians 3:2** and later in that letter he writes "11 And you know that we treated each of you as a father treats his own children. 12 We pleaded with you, encouraged you, and urged you to live your lives in a way that God would consider worthy. For he called you to share in his Kingdom and glory. **1 Thessalonians 2:11-12.**

Our God is a God who encourages and there are examples of this throughout the Bible. Just one example of this was when God encouraged Joshua to take over from Moses as leader of the Israelites (**Joshua 1:19**). In Paul's second letter to the Thessalonians he also writes about God encouraging his people. "May our Lord Jesus Christ himself and God our Father, who loved us and by his grace gave us eternal encouragement and good hope, [17] encourage your hearts and strengthen you in every good deed and word." **2 Thessalonians 2:16-17** (NIV).

When we give others encouragement it helps them to continue in their Christian journey, it strengthens their resolve and commitment to their faith. When we encourage them in how they are seeking to use the gifts and talents God has given them, it affirms for them that they are doing what God has called them to do and it strengthens them in their service. Encouragement helps people to live courageously, it helps them to persevere during times of difficulty, it encourages them to continue to be obedient to God and it comforts them in times of trouble.

It costs us very little effort to encourage another person when compared with how much it means to the one who receives the encouragement. Let's determine together to be regular encouragers.

To Think About:

- *What has it meant to you when someone has taken the time to encourage you?*

- *Who has God used to be an encouragement to you? Take some time in prayer thanking God for that person in your life.*

- *Ask God this coming week to place on your heart someone who is in need of encouragement, and ask him to show you how best you can encourage them.*

A Rainbow Moment

Dear Friend,

I get a thrill every time I see a rainbow, just as much now as I did when I was a child. I just can't help it, it fills me with joy and wonder, and an "Oh wow!" escapes my lips. There's something so special about a rainbow, with its colours and perfectly created arc shape in the sky.

My family and I were travelling home having spent a lovely weekend with my sister and her family. It was late Monday morning following one of the biggest storms we have experienced for some years. The worst of the storm was over, but the sky was still overcast, it was cold, windy and at times there was heavy rain.

Then, in the midst of this, the sun came out from behind the clouds and a beautiful rainbow appeared. We saw it from one end of the bow to the other. I'm so glad I was awake to see it (often the motion of the car ride sends me off to sleep!)

It was back in the time of a man called Noah after he and his family survived the flood whilst in the ark, when God first made a rainbow as a sign to Noah that he would never again flood the whole world. It's a promise that God made and has kept ever since. "Then God said, "I am giving you a sign of my covenant with you and with all living creatures, for all generations to come. I have placed my rainbow in the clouds. It is the sign of my covenant with you and with all the earth. When I send clouds over the earth, the rainbow will appear in the clouds, and I will remember my covenant with you and with all living creatures. Never again will the floodwaters destroy all life. When I see the rainbow in the clouds, I will remember the eternal covenant between God and every living creature on earth." **Genesis 9:12-16.** It's not just that the rainbow is a thing of beauty created by God which holds an attraction for me: it's also because when I see a rainbow it reminds me that God is faithful, that he is a maker and keeper of promises and for me it's a reminder that he is present in the world today.

At one time or another we will all face the storms of life, these storms vary in length and intensity and can come from a variety of sources, such as facing a serious illness, a financial crisis, a marriage breakdown, the loss of a loved one, unemployment, a rebellious child etc. But I believe that in these storms God sends us "a rainbow moment" when we get a glimpse of his presence with us in the storm and he reminds us that we're not facing the storm alone. He cares and he's right there with us, proving his faithfulness once again to us. He reminds us that he will keep the promises he's made to us, that we will come through the storm, we won't be blown over and we won't be consumed by it because he will give us the power and strength we need to stand and to stand firm!

God says to each one of us "When you go through deep waters, I will be with you. When you go through rivers of difficulty, you will not drown. When you walk through the fire of oppression, you will not be burned up; the flames will not consume you. For I am the Lord, your God, the Holy One of Israel, your Saviour." **Isaiah 43:2-3**

Peter gives this word of encouragement to his readers: "Stay alert! Watch out for your great enemy, the devil. He prowls around like a roaring lion, looking for someone to devour. Stand firm against him, and be strong in your faith. Remember that your

Christian brothers and sisters all over the world are going through the same kind of suffering you are." **1 Peter 5: 8-9**

These "rainbow moments" don't necessarily need to take place in a church building, although they may do as we gather with our church family. A "rainbow moment" can happen through a worship song you hear on a CD, during a time of quiet alone with God, through a passage of the Bible. You may experience it whilst out for a walk along the beach. It can be seen when your husband comes home with a bunch of flowers for you...when you share a precious moment with your child as you settle them down for the night... when a friend invites you out for a coffee, or phones you because they felt God prompting them to ring you, although they didn't know why. These are special "rainbow moments" when God, via a variety of means, connects with you in your storm to remind you that he knows, and more importantly he cares. He has not left you alone, he is with you always and that this storm, like any other, will pass.

But these special "rainbow moments" can easily be missed by us. Just as I would have missed the rainbow last Monday morning if I had been sleeping. If we are too focused on the storm itself - the darkness that's trying to consume us, the wind trying to knock us down and keep us down, the rain trying to flood us and make us feel like we're drowning in the onslaught - then we fail to recognise and fail to see God's "rainbow moment" he's created especially for us.

As we continue to seek God, to believe in his faithfulness and love for us, as we spend time in his presence, praying and reading the bible, we will be more tuned in to him, and more aware so that we can learn to see and recognise these "rainbow moments".

To Think About:

- *Look back over the storms of your life. As you do so, can you recognise any "rainbow moments" God has given you?*

- *Are you in a storm right now? Ask God to help you see his presence with you and ask him for a "rainbow moment".*

- *It may be that God wants you to be that "rainbow moment" in the life of another person. Listen to the promptings he places in your heart and thoughts and then do something about with it.*

"Following My Leader"

Dear Friend,

At the school my children attend they are re-introducing the prefect system. (Make sure you read that correctly the prefect system not perfect system!!) Whereas in the past, most Year 11 (final year of secondary school) students were prefects, this time there is a process to go through and if the student is successful then he/she is given the position of prefect.

Josh has decided to apply to be a prefect and has submitted his application form. The next stage will involve an interview and then there's a third stage before the final decision is made. Now, I know that Josh would make an excellent prefect - he is hard working, he has good relationships with staff and his peers, and I can remember him telling me a year or so ago how his friends (boys and girls) would come to him for advice if they'd got any problems. He would be a great role model for the younger students and be an influence for good. To be selected for the role of prefect is a privilege and a responsibility. A privilege because not everyone is suited to it and a responsibility because others will be watching more closely. If they see a prefect with a bad attitude, or misbehaving or speaking in a wrong manner, students will think if it's ok for him then it's ok for them and the prefect will have a bad influence on them, but if the prefect sets a good example they can influence others for good.

I'm reminded of what Paul writes in **1 Corinthians 11: 1** "Pattern yourselves after me [follow my example], as I imitate and follow Christ (the Messiah)." (Amplified Bible)

Earlier in his life Paul wrote in another letter "So you received the message with joy from the Holy Spirit in spite of the severe suffering it brought you. In this way, you imitated both us and the Lord. As a result, you have become an example to all the believers in Greece—throughout both Macedonia and Achaia." **1 Thessalonians 1:6-8**

As a child I used to play the game "Follow my leader". One child was chosen to be the leader and the rest of us would follow them, copying them wherever they went. If you couldn't see the leader then you could copy the child in front who you hoped was doing a good job of copying the leader. It meant watching very closely so you didn't miss what was happening.

As Christians we are to follow, copy, imitate the example of Jesus Christ. If we are going to do this well then we need to keep in close step with him, spend time with him and study the Bible. It can also help to build up a close relationship with a mature Christian who you trust, and watch their behaviour, the way they speak, how they respond in different situations. It can also be helpful to talk with them and ask them questions to learn more about how to live the Christian life.

As Christians we are to be an example to others, just as the Thessalonians were an example to other believers in Greece. Imitating Christ is also a good way to point others to him. We can influence people more by the way we live, rather than by just telling them about Christ.

It can be quite daunting. What happens when I mess up, what kind of example is that to others? Well, we're not perfect (only Christ lived a perfect life on earth) and the truth is we will at times get things wrong, we will mess up, we will sin. However, we can still be an example to others as they watch how we respond to our mistakes, such as when we've lost our temper or hurt someone by our actions, what do we do to restore our relationship with them? We need to be open about our need to confess to God when we have sinned and seek his forgiveness. It helps others to then know that there is something positive to do when they have sinned. That there is restoration for our relationships both with God and others, and that just because they have messed up it does not mean they can no longer follow Christ.

There will always be people in our life who we have an influence over, such as our children, our husband, close friend, work colleague, a younger Christian. It's not about saying to them, "Hey, look at me, I'm such a good Christian." Rather, we do things in such a way so we are reflecting Christ and pointing them to God, so that they see him in us. John the Baptist said of Jesus: "He must become greater; I must become less."
John 3:30 (NIV)

Let's commit to following, copying, imitating Christ and in doing so let's make sure our influence is for good so that others will want to copy our example and so that God is glorified.

To Think About:

- *What does it mean to you to imitate Christ?*

- *Who has been the biggest help and influence in your Christian journey so far? Why is that and how have they done this?*

- *As you practice what you have learned, who is there in your life right now who would benefit from having you as their role model?*

A Spiritual Health Check

Dear Friend,

This week I was given a free NHS Health Check. The check is offered to everyone between the ages of 40 and 74 and is part of a national scheme to help prevent the onset of health problems such as heart disease, type 2 diabetes, kidney disease and stroke and helps you to "be better prepared for the future and be able to take steps to maintain or improve your health." I had a blood test to check my cholesterol level, my blood pressure was taken and my height and weight measured. I was declared healthy in regards to those health problems and encouraged to maintain my health with a healthy diet and exercise.

This physical health check got me thinking and I made the decision this week to have a spiritual health check too. Just as I needed the help of a professional to take me through my physical, I knew I wasn't qualified to do my spiritual health check on my own - I needed the help of the Holy Spirit to take me through it as he is the one who can help me identify any areas of concern and he is also able to help me deal with them so that I can maintain and improve my spiritual health.

So with the Holy Spirit and God's Word I attended my personal spiritual health check and have outlined the process on the following page:

Prayer: "Search me, O God, and know my heart; test me and know my anxious thoughts. Point out anything in me that offends you, and lead me along the path of everlasting life." **Psalm 139:23-24**

1.　　**My Heart:** Do I have a servant heart? Do I love the things God loves? Is God at the centre of my heart? Am I harbouring any unhealthy feelings that need to be dealt with, such as anger, fear, worry, bitterness, pride, unforgiveness, jealousy?

Prayer: "Create in me a clean heart, O God. Renew a loyal spirit within me." **Psalm 51:10**

2.　　**My Mind:** this concerns my thought life. What occupies my mind? What kinds of things am I allowing my mind to dwell on - are they healthy or unhealthy things?   Do I have any unhealthy attitudes?

3. **My Mouth:** What kind of speech comes out of my mouth?
Do I gossip? Lie? Boast? Discourage? Criticise? Is my speech judgmental? Or do I speak words of encouragement? Words that are loving and compassionate? Uplifting? Truthful? Words that give praise to God? Jesus said "A good person produces good things from the treasury of a good heart, and an evil person produces evil things from the treasury of an evil heart. What you say flows from what is in your heart." **Luke 6:45.** The things I say give me a good indication as to the spiritual health of my heart.

Prayer: "May the words of my mouth and the meditation of my heart be pleasing to you, O Lord, my rock and my redeemer." **Psalm 19:14**

4. **My Hands and Feet:** this concerns my actions. What am I doing with my time? Do I use it wisely? Am I seeking to do God's will? Is

there an area of my life where I am being disobedient to God? Is there any unhealthy behaviour in my life?

Prayer: "Thank you God that you have begun a good work in me, and thank you that you will continue your work in my life until it is completed when Jesus returns." (based on **Philippians 1:6**)

With the Holy Spirit's guidance, I went through each of the four areas I've mentioned. Whenever he pointed out sin in my life, I confessed it, repented of it and asked for God's forgiveness. He showed me areas where I needed to change and promised he would help me. And he also showed me areas where I was to maintain, with his help, my spiritual health.

At the end of my physical health check I asked the nurse when my next one would be, only to be told that this was a one-off free health check. I'm so glad a spiritual health check isn't a one-off. It is necessary that you and I regularly set aside time with God to examine the state of our spiritual health, so that the Holy Spirit can reveal to us anything unhealthy, and then our health can be restored as we work with him, following his leading and guidance. Our spiritual health is maintained by keeping a close relationship with God and allowing him to speak into our life, by regularly reading the Bible (a healthy diet) and by applying it to our lives and putting it into practice (healthy exercise).

To Think About:

- *Make time in the next week or so to have your own spiritual health check. You may want to use what I've shared as a starting point or you may feel led by God to do it differently.*

- *The nurse I saw gave me a record of her findings. If you keep a journal you may find it helpful to keep a record of your spiritual health check so when you repeat it, you have something to compare it with.*

Christ's Personal Representative

Dear Friend,

In **Ephesians 4:1** (NIV) Paul urges us "to live a life worthy of the calling you have received". Paul writes in **2 Corinthians 5:20** that our calling is to follow Christ and be his ambassadors, or as the Amplified Bible puts it "Christ's personal representatives".

That's quite a privilege and a responsibility, isn't it? I need to remember as I go about my daily business, that I'm Christ's personal representative. I am to represent him in the things I say and do.

This week I needed to go to my local pharmacy to collect and pay for some of Jason's and my prescriptions. Now, I'm no maths genius but I could tell from the figure the chemist gave me that she had totalled it up wrongly, she had missed off the cost of one of the prescriptions. As a follower of Christ and one of his representatives, I knew that I needed to point out that she had undercharged me. She thanked me for my honesty and seemed surprised I had pointed out her mistake to her.

In any situation we face, you and I, as Christ's ambassadors, have a choice to make regarding our actions and speech. In my encounter with the chemist I could have chosen not to reveal to her that a mistake had been made. It may be tempting to think, "I'm not hurting anyone, it's the cashier's fault, no-one will know about it" or "I'm glad she got it wrong, money's been tight this month". But even though it was the cashier who had made the mistake, for me to keep quiet about it is dishonest and stealing. Not great for a representative of Christ, is it? I can tell myself, "Nobody is hurt by this", but the truth is that others <u>are</u> hurt by it, and more importantly God is grieved over my actions, I've sinned and I too am hurt by my actions as it damages my relationship with God. Whilst others may not find out about my dishonest actions, I will always know and God definitely knows. We can't hide anything from him. When I make the right choices I am representing Christ in such a way that brings glory to God.

God has provided us with the power and the authority to be Christ's representative to the world by giving us his Holy Spirit. We need to listen to his voice as he prompts us to certain actions, as he prompts us in what to say, and as he guides us against other actions. The more we listen to him and follow his guidance, the more familiar we will be with his voice and the easier it gets to recognise him. The opposite is also true, when we resist his leading and direction time after time, choosing our own way, it becomes less easy to hear and recognise his voice.

As Christ's ambassadors we are here to give an accurate representation of who Christ is. We need to make sure that we are portraying Christ well to those who don't yet know him. We are his representative at all times, wherever we are and whomever we are with; whether at home as we take care of family, at work with our colleagues, at church, socialising with friends, waiting in a queue or chatting with neighbours. They need to see Christ in us so that we can share with them the good news of knowing Christ for themselves. As Christ's representatives we are to share his message of peace and reconciliation with God.

If we are to accurately represent Christ to the world, then we need to know him well ourselves. Christ is not to be some passing acquaintance, or a distant relative whom we see every now and again. We're to know him as we know our closest friends, to know him in depth just as we know our husband or wife. The only way that we will truly know Christ is by spending time with him, quality time with him, not a few minutes grabbed here and there.

> **To Think About:**
>
> - *Do you know Christ well enough that you are able to give an accurate representation of him? If the answer is no, what will you do to change this?*
>
> - *When is it easier to represent him and when is it harder? Ask God for his help, especially when it is hard.*
>
> - *In what area of your life do you think God may be challenging you to become a better representative? Will you take up the challenge?*

Where Is God When I'm Hurting?
(Part 1)

Dear Friend,

We recently had our bi-annual family outing to the dentist. I don't mind having a check-up at the dentist; to tell you the truth, I'd rather have a dental appointment than an appointment with the doctor. My daughter, Jess, on the other hand, does not like visiting the dentist.

At this particular appointment the dentist wanted to clean her teeth as there was a build-up of plaque. If she was tense before that comment, she was even more tense now, especially when he told her to just lift her hand if it got too painful. As I sat watching the proceedings I could tell she was anxious, scared and in pain at times. Now, the casual observer would not have picked up on it, but, as her mother, and knowing her so well, I knew exactly how she was feeling.

I found it very hard to sit and watch my little girl suffering (at 12 years old she doesn't like me calling her that, but that's what she is to me!) and my natural instinct as her Mum was to do anything I could to protect her. But, at the same time, I knew that she needed to sit there and experience the painful situation, it was in her best interests as she would then have healthier teeth and gums. Knowing that did not make it any easier for me. So I did the one thing I was able to do for her, I prayed for her.

We too face, at one time or another, difficulties and trials; in fact, you may be in the middle of one right now. We want God to act, to do something to alleviate the pain, to stop whatever it is that's causing us anxiety and hurt. But when he doesn't, we think he doesn't care about us or he would do something. He can't really love us; if he did, surely he would act? We may think like that, but that's not the truth. God does care and he does love us. In **Nahum 1:7** it says "The Lord is good, a refuge in times of trouble. He cares for those who trust in him," (NIV)

In his letter to the Ephesians Paul writes "Then Christ will make his home in your hearts as you trust in him. Your roots will grow down into God's love and keep you strong. 18 And may you have the power to understand, as all God's people should, how wide, how long, how high, and how deep his love is. 19 May you experience the love of Christ, though it is too great to understand fully. Then you will be made complete with all the fullness of life and power that comes from God." **Ephesians 3:17-19**. These are important truths for us to hang on to when we listen to the Devil's lies and begin to doubt God's love for us.

God's truth is for each one who puts their trust in him and to really grasp hold of the truth it can be helpful to personalise it by putting yourself into the verse. God wants you to know that what he is saying is for you, right now, whatever your circumstances. Let me give you an example: **Romans 8:38-39** could be reworded as:

"And I, Vicki, am convinced that nothing can ever separate me from God's love. Neither death nor life, neither angels nor demons, neither my fears for today nor my worries about tomorrow—not even the powers of hell can separate me from God's love. 39 No power in the sky above or in the earth below— indeed, nothing in all creation will ever be able to separate me from the love of God that is revealed in Christ Jesus my Lord." It really brings it home for me, yes God is saying this to everyone who believes in him, and yes, there's the sense that he's also saying it just for me too!

I can remember some verses more easily than others because I've known and loved them for years, but for those I don't remember I have a habit of writing them on card or paper and putting them near my bedside table where I can see and read them regularly. It's a great place for me as I spend quite a bit of time in my bedroom. We need to know and be reminded of the truth, especially when going through pain and difficulties.

Another verse that means a great deal to me and proves to me that God cares is this: "You (God) keep track of all my sorrows. You have collected all my tears in your bottle. You have recorded each one in your book." **Psalm 56:8**. This verse is precious to me because it shows me that God is close enough to me to hear and see what I'm going through, he cares enough to collect my tears in a bottle and he is right there with me. He's been with me as I've cried because of my depression, when I've cried because of pain and frustration and when I've cried when no-one else has been around to hear. This brings me such comfort.

God does love and care for us and he is with us as we face pain and difficulties; whether we do or don't feel his presence with us does not alter the truth that he is there. Just as I was with Jess all the time she sat in the dentist's chair, she may not have been fully aware I was there, because she was wrapped up in what she was going through, but I was there just the same, and I was praying for her.

To Think About:

- *If you're facing a difficult time right now, ask God to help you know he is with you in the midst of the trial and that he loves and cares for you.*

- *Consider putting verses that encourage you on card and placing them where you will see them often throughout the day, e.g. your kitchen fridge, in your wallet, on the dashboard of your car etc. Pray them when you are struggling to believe God's truth over the devil's lies.*

- *Why not take a verse that is encouraging to you and personalise it yourself, just as I did with Romans 8:38-39. Does it change the way you think and understand that verse?*

Where Is God When I'm Hurting?
(Part 2)

Dear Friend,

Last week I wrote that we can know, even during our trials, that God loves us, cares about us and is with us in our pain. You may remember I shared about Jess' experience at the dentist, that it was painful to endure it, but that it was in her best interests she did so.

God, our loving heavenly Father, sometimes allows us to go through difficult and painful circumstances because they are ultimately for our good. He uses these times to grow our faith in him, to deepen our trust, and to take us on in our Christian journey. For example, James says to his readers "Dear brothers and sisters, when troubles come your way, consider it an opportunity for great joy. ³ For you know that when your faith is tested, your endurance has a chance to grow. ⁴ So let it grow, for when your endurance is fully developed, you will be perfect and complete, needing nothing." **James 1:2-4.**

Be encouraged that whatever difficult and painful time you are going through, whatever trial you are facing - which shows no sign of ending no matter how much you pray - God will be using it for your good. Now, I know you may not want to hear that right now, but I do believe there will come a time, perhaps when you have come through the other side, that you will be able to see that God was able to bring something good from it. When you look to God and trust him, none trial will be wasted.

Did you want to skim over the first verse I mentioned? James tells us that we are to see the trial as an opportunity for great joy. Really, James? Yes, really! But let me clarify what he means - James is not saying rejoice in the trial itself, the breakdown of a relationship, financial difficulties, redundancy, miscarriage, chronic illness etc. - that would be crazy. But we can, when we trust and lean on God, have joy in who our God is and all he has done for us, all he has given us and all he is doing in us. It doesn't mean we are in denial as we go through the trial, but it does mean instead of being focused on the trial itself, we focus on God.

The experiences Paul wrote about in his letters which are written about him in the book of Acts have given me much encouragement in the past, and continue to do so today. He experienced persecution, torture, floggings, shipwrecks and imprisonment. In his second letter to the Corinthians he wrote about his thorn in the flesh, something that was giving him considerable torment and was the cause of much personal suffering. We don't know exactly what his thorn in the flesh was, but not knowing what it was actually helps us to relate his difficulty to whatever we are suffering. This is what he wrote about it *"Three different times I begged the Lord to take it away. 9 Each time he said, 'My grace is all you need. My power works best in weakness.' So now I am glad to boast about my weaknesses, so that the power of Christ can work through me. 10 That's why I take pleasure in my weaknesses, and in the insults, hardships, persecutions, and troubles that I suffer for Christ. For when I am weak, then I am strong."* **2 Corinthians 12:8-10.**

In the midst of our difficulties, our hurts, God is right there and we have the wonderful promise that his grace is sufficient for us. It's God's grace that enables us to bear up under the weight of the trial so we are not overcome by it. The truth is God's power works best in our weakness and we can be strong because of God's power in us. I can testify to the truth of this. There have been numerous times in my life when God has worked despite my weaknesses or perhaps even because of them. When I acknowledge to him that I am too weak, that I have limitations, that I need to depend and rely on him, then I give him the opportunity and room to work through me. My illness is a constant reminder I can do nothing without him and at the same time can do all that he has planned for me to do because he is working in me, giving me the strength I need. I find that incredible and so encouraging. The truth of those verses never gets old to me: every time I read them or think about them I get a thrill from deep within my very being, and within I shout "Amen! Hallelujah!"

I like the way The Message paraphrases these verses (v7-10): "Because of the extravagance of those revelations, and so I wouldn't get a big head, I was given the gift of a handicap to keep me in constant touch with my limitations. Satan's angel did his best to get me down; what he in fact did was push me to my knees. No danger then of walking around high and mighty! At first I didn't think of it as a gift, and begged God to remove it. Three times I did that, and then he told me, 'My grace is enough; it's all you need. My strength comes into its own in your weakness.' Once I heard that, I was glad to let it happen. I quit focusing on the handicap and began appreciating the gift. It was a case of Christ's strength moving in on my weakness. Now I take limitations in stride, and with good cheer, these limitations that cut me down to size—abuse, accidents, opposition, bad breaks. I just let Christ take over! And so the weaker I get, the stronger I become."

Be encouraged dear friends, God is with you when you're hurting and he can and will use these times for good. Joseph was able to say to his brothers, years after the hurt they had caused him, "19 But Joseph replied, 'Don't be afraid of me. Am I God, that I can punish you? ²⁰ You intended to harm me, but God intended it all for good." **Genesis 50:19-20a**.

Not only is God with us, we can also know the gift of his grace which enables us to withstand and overcome the trial.

To Think About:

- *Read Joseph's story in **Genesis 37**, **39-50** to learn how Joseph was able to say what he did in **Genesis 50:19-20a**. What can you learn from his example?*

- *Can you look back over your life and see how God has taken what was a bad experience and has brought good from it?*

- *Do you experience times when you recognise you are weak and need to rely on his strength to enable you to serve him and times when you experience his grace working in you? What are the results of depending on him?*

A King Worthy of Our Worship

Dear Friend,

Over the past few weeks my family and I have been watching "I'm a celebrity...get me out of here!" We've watched as a group of celebrities who don't know each other are dropped off in the Australian jungle for a few weeks. They take little with them into the camp; they sleep on camp beds and cook basic food on the camp fire. They take part in various gruesome trials and face elimination from the jungle by public vote until just one person, the winner, is left. The one who is the last to leave is crowned King (or Queen) of the Jungle. Although they may not all admit to it, they have selfish reasons for participating in this reality TV show, whether it's money, or to further their careers or to win public approval. To some people it would be viewed as quite a feat as the celebrities face and survive the jungle, with one person winning the victory by lasting the longest.

But, I know of one who has done something far more incredible and it's good for us to be reminded of it at this time of year.

Of course, I'm thinking about Jesus Christ, the Son of God, who gave up his place in heaven, his position, everything, to come to earth, to be born in a place reserved for animals, with a feeding trough as his first bed. **Philippians 2:6-7** says this "Though he was God, he did not think of equality with God as something to cling to. 7 Instead, he gave up his divine privileges, he took the humble position of a slave and was born as a human being."

He did this, not for some selfish reason and not to win people's approval (actually the religious leaders at that time definitely disapproved of him and hated him, even going as far as manipulating the situation to have him killed). Jesus came to earth for purely unselfish reasons. He came to restore our relationship to God, to take the punishment we deserve for our sins and to bring us life, peace, hope, love and joy, and to show us what God the Father is like.

At the time of Jesus' birth an angel appeared to shepherds. "Don't be afraid!' he said. 'I bring you good news that will bring great joy to all people. 11 The Saviour—yes, the Messiah, the Lord—has been born today in Bethlehem, the city of David! 12 And you will recognize him by this sign: You will find a baby wrapped snugly in strips of cloth, lying in a manger.' 13 Suddenly, the angel was joined by a vast host of others—the armies of heaven—praising God and saying, 14 'Glory to God in highest heaven, and peace on earth to those with whom God is pleased.'" **Luke 2:10-14**.

The trials the celebrities faced in the jungle were nothing compared to the trials Jesus endured as he walked this earth for about thirty-three years. The greatest trial he faced and overcame was death on a cross. The passage we read in **Philippians** continues in **verse 8** with "he humbled himself in obedience to God and died a criminal's death on a cross." Jesus Christ went to the cross for my sake, for your sake, because "God so greatly loved and dearly prized the world that He [even] gave up His only begotten (unique) Son, so that whoever believes in (trusts in, clings to, relies on) Him shall not perish (come to destruction, be lost) but have eternal (everlasting) life." **John 3:16** (Amplified Bible)

Jesus was victorious, he defeated the devil and his plans. He overcame death, our final enemy: "54 Then, when our dying bodies have been transformed into bodies that will never die, this

Scripture will be fulfilled: 'Death is swallowed up in victory. 55 O death, where is your victory? O death, where is your sting?'" **1 Corinthians 15:54-56.**

The last celebrity remaining in the jungle is crowned King (or Queen) of the Jungle. In reality, this means very little. However, Jesus, our victor is crowned King of Kings and Lord of Lords. "For at just the right time Christ will be revealed from heaven by the blessed and only almighty God, the King of all kings and Lord of all lords." **1 Timothy 6:15**. As such, he alone is worthy of our worship and adoration.

Let's go back to **Philippians 2** and read **verses 9-11** "Therefore, God elevated him to the place of highest honour and gave him the name above all other names, 10 that at the name of Jesus every knee should bow, in heaven and on earth and under the earth, 11 and every tongue confess that Jesus Christ is Lord, to the glory of God the Father."

As we look forward to Christmas let's remember all that Jesus Christ gave up to come to earth, to live as a man, so we might be reconciled with God and have eternal life. As we celebrate Jesus' birth, we can also worship him as King and Lord of our life.

To Think About:

- *Make time during the coming week to worship Jesus our King and Saviour.*

- *God has given us the greatest gift of all, his son, Jesus. What will you give to God in response to this gift?*

Jesus Christ - The Reason for the Season

Dear Friend,

"Look! The virgin will conceive a child! She will give birth to a son and they will call him Immanuel which means 'God is with us'."
Matthew 1:23

What a great name 'Immanuel' is - 'God is with us'. Jesus Christ came to live among us and he is the reason why we celebrate Christmas. What an incredible, indescribable gift God gave to us on that first Christmas, over 2000 years ago. God has given us the gift of Jesus so we might know what it means to have God with us, to know his presence which never leaves us. To know he is with us and he is for us, not against us, which means we are blessed not only by his presence but also by his protection over us.

This year as I prepare for Christmas I've been more deliberate about keeping Jesus Christ as my focus and at the centre of everything I do, rather than focusing on what I think needs to be done. When I'm not deliberate about it then I find I easily become caught up in the hustle and bustle of Christmas - shopping for gifts, planning the menus, food shopping, sending cards and letters etc. And the one who it is all about, the one whose birthday we celebrate is relegated to the side lines, rather than being at the centre of it all.

Here are some of the things I've been doing, and maybe you'll find some helpful suggestions for yourself as you read on:

I enjoy music and singing (I may not be any good at it but God has blessed me with an enjoyment of it!) so in November, out come my Christmas Carol CDs, they are set to come on when my alarm goes off in the morning. I sing along to them as I drive my car, I play them and sing along as I do my housework, as I wrap presents and write my Christmas cards.

I found out about a Ladies Christmas Celebration Day early in December and a group of friends and I put aside the day to go together to worship God. All the things we needed to do were left for another time so we could focus on God and the birth of his son, Jesus. We sang carols, listened to a message about Elizabeth (the mother of John the Baptist) and her Christmas Expectations, and we enjoyed a festive lunch together. This day was God's gift to us, and in return, we gave him our time and worship.

One day last week I went into town to do some Christmas shopping, but it wasn't long before I was in need of a break so I decided to go along to my favourite coffee place. While I was there, I realised to my surprise that a Christian friend of mine was already seated with her own coffee. I knew God had led me there at that time so that my friend and I might sit and chat together, and as we did so I was aware of God being right there with us in our conversation. God had given us that time that we might pause and refocus on him and to remind us he is right there with us in everything we do, directing our steps, and both my friend and I went away from that time feeling very blessed.

In one of my regular devotional emails I receive the writer made the suggestion of praying during the week for each of the people we give Christmas presents to. I thought it was such a good idea and I was glad for the suggestion, so simple and obvious when told, but something I had failed to see for myself.

This morning I was so taken up with the list of things needing to be done today (I'm very much a list person and this time of year I have numerous lists for all kinds of things!) I knew my feelings of anxiety and worry were getting out of hand, so I just stopped everything and took my concerns to God. I knew I was in danger of getting so swept up in trying to accomplish things that I was losing my peace and joy and if I wasn't careful God would once again be placed on the side lines rather than at the centre. As I did, it made such a difference: my To Do list didn't disappear but my attitude changed, and God was right where he should be once more.

This Christmas I don't want it to be all about what I think needs to be done. I don't want to be so busy I ignore God or forget him. I don't want it to be all about rushing from one task to another. I don't want to miss out on what it's really all about - the wonderful gift of Jesus and celebrating his birth with family and friends.

To Think About:

- *What are some of the things you can do to ensure that Jesus is at the centre of your Christmas?*

- *Sometimes we get caught up in doing many things which may not actually need to be done, but we do them because we think we ought to, because we think we should do them, and we place pressure on ourselves that God never intended to be on us.*

- *Perhaps you need to take a look again at what you are doing and ask God to show you if there are some things that can be left off your "To Do" list, so you can use that time to be with friends and family and celebrate Jesus' birth.*

Looking Ahead

Dear Friend,

As we are coming to the end of the year, I find my thoughts going to the New Year which will soon be upon us. Over the last week or so I began to think about "What do I want for this coming year?" What are my hopes, my dreams, my goals for the coming year? That is, until God showed me it was the wrong question to be asking. You see, it's not about me and what I want; instead it's all about God and what he wants for me. What does God want for me, for you, in this year to come?

It's all very well looking ahead considering what goals and aims I may have, but if I ignore God in my deliberations then my goals and aims will come to nothing. **Proverbs 19:21** tells us "Many are the plans in a person's heart, but it is the Lord's purpose that prevails." (NIV) and in **Proverbs 16:9** "We can make our plans, but the Lord determines our steps." When we allow God to determine the direction we take then we will have success.

So, I've begun to set aside time over the next few weeks when I can be alone with God and focus on him. I want to reflect on what's happened during the last year, and for this I'm glad I have kept a journal. My journal reminds me of the things I have learnt, the direction God has taken me thus far and how he has been preparing me for another year. In the times I set aside to be alone with God I would like him to reveal to me the things he wants me to continue with and develop and the things he is telling me to let go of, to leave behind.

Paul writes in **Philippians 3:12-14** "Yet, my brothers, I do not consider myself to have "arrived", spiritually, nor do I consider myself already perfect. But I keep going on, grasping ever more firmly that purpose for which Christ grasped me. My brothers, I do not consider myself to have fully grasped it even now. But I do concentrate on this: I leave the past behind and with hands outstretched to whatever lies ahead I go straight for the goal—my reward the honour of being called by God in Christ." (PHILLIPS)

As I look ahead I'm enquiring of God what his purpose is for me for this year. What direction does he want me to go in? How can I align myself with him, so that his plan for me becomes my plan too? Is there something new he wants me to do? Are there things he wants me to continue in, to develop and grow in certain areas? What are the desires he has already placed in my heart? What goals does he want me to focus on? While some goals may be achievable short term, others may be more long term before fruition is seen and it's important to know the difference. God has created you and me, and he has created us for a purpose, so if we want to know what that is, we need to take the time to ask him. We need a sense of direction which only God can give. When you know what God wants you to do and an opportunity presents itself - if it is something that takes you nearer to God's plans for you - you can embrace it.

God is Lord of my whole life, not just the part that's reserved for Sunday mornings. Because he is Lord of my life I want to know what he wants for me in all areas of my life - in my relationship with him, in my roles of wife and mother and in my ministry.

As I mentioned earlier, I keep a journal. I plan to use it to record all God has shown me, the plans, goals and aims he sets within me and what he wants me to do. The time I spend with God at the beginning of this new year will give me a sense of direction and purpose for the rest of the year. Having these things written down means I can return to it whenever I want to.

It's about keeping my focus on God and his purpose for me. This is what will help me to keep to the path he has set before me and it will help me to keep pursuing it even when it gets difficult or I doubt myself. **Hebrews 12:1-2** "And let us run with endurance the race God has set before us. We do this by keeping our eyes on Jesus, the champion who initiates and perfects our faith."

One thing that has already come out of the time I have spent with God is that during this coming year I want to read through the whole of the Bible again. It's been some years since I read it through and this year I want to read it in a chronological Bible. It will probably be a good idea to choose someone I can be accountable to, who will encourage me and also give me a nudge when I need it to keep going.

To Think About:

- *Set aside some time to review this current year. What new things have you learnt about God? What direction has he taken you in? How has God shown you he loves you and is with you?*

- *Make time to enquire of God what he wants for you in this coming year. Record it in the way you prefer so that you can refer to it over the coming months.*

About the Author

I live in the South East of England with my husband, Jason and our two teenage children, Joshua and Jessica.

We attend Gateway Christian Church where Jason is the Assistant Minister and I am on the preaching/teaching team.

God has blessed me with a love for His Word, for studying it and for sharing His Word with others. He has also given me a joy of writing. This led me a few years ago to start my devotional blog, "Hope for Today" and from this grew my desire to have a paperback devotional book published. This book is a result of this dream.

If you would like to connect with me there are various ways you can do so:
- subscribe to my blog, "Hope for Today": http://vickicottingham.blogspot.co.uk/
- follow me on twitter: @vickicotting14
- https://www.facebook.com/vickicottingham14/

Printed in Poland
by Amazon Fulfillment
Poland Sp. z o.o., Wrocław

54909479R00105